Revenue Management, Cost Control, and Financial Analysis in the Hospitality Industry

First Edition

By Godwin-Charles Ogbeide
University of Arkansas – Fayetteville

cognella®
academic publishing

Bassim Hamadeh, CEO and Publisher
Michael Simpson, Vice President of Acquisitions
Jamie Giganti, Managing Editor
Jess Busch, Graphic Design Supervisor
Becky Smith, Acquisitions Editor
Monika Dziamka, Project Editor
Natalie Lakosil, Licensing Manager
Mandy Licata, Interior Designer

First published in the United States of America in 2014 by Cognella, Inc.

Cover credits: Copyright © 2011 by Depositphotos Inc./Ling Pui Yee; Copyright © 2010 by Depositphotos Inc./Dmitri Mihhailov; Copyright © 2012 by Depositphotos Inc./Robert Lerich; Copyright © 2011 by Depositphotos Inc./Олъга Кригер

Printed in the United States of America

ISBN: 978-1-62661-752-0 (pbk)/ 978-1-62661-753-7 (br)

www.cognella.com   800-200-3908

Contents

CHAPTER 1: INTRODUCTION TO FINANCIAL ANALYSIS AND SPREADSHEET MODELING

CHAPTER 2: ACCOUNTING OPERATIONS IN THE HOSPITALITY INDUSTRY

CHAPTER 6: BUDGETING

CHAPTER 7: REVENUE MANAGEMENT

PREFACE

Effective hospitality managers, alongside managers in any industry, have many abilities, including accounting and financial skills. In the hospitality industry, the importance of accounting concepts and financial analysis in the daily operation of the revenue centers (i.e., restaurants, front office, retail stores, etc.) cannot be overemphasized. Accounting and financial analysis deals with numbers, which are used in measuring an organization's performance in achieving its financial goals. Not all managers, however, enjoy the complexity of accounting and financial subjects. This book simplifies the accounting and financial principles needed by managers in their organization's daily operations. Generally speaking, profitability is a common measure of any organization's success. Effective managers understand that cost must be rationally controlled in order to be profitable. In addition to cost control, effective managers understand the importance of utilizing revenue management principles for maximizing revenues while supplying the same quantity of product. If revenue is maximized and cost is controlled to its lowest rational level, profit will be maximized.

This textbook has been developed to provide students, future managers, and managers with the necessary skills needed to control costs and maximize revenues without the unnecessary complex accounting skills. It combined basic accounting skills with the spreadsheet modeling of financial statements. This is a simplified way to use Microsoft Excel or any other spreadsheet to design and analyze financial statements. This book also provides a step-by-step approach to various examples of financial statements including budgeting, a critical responsibility of effective managers.

The author of this book has previously innovated this course by incorporating the spreadsheet-modeling approach to the financial analysis in his hospitality operations and financial analysis course. The author significantly changed the course from a lecture-based course to include hands-on, spreadsheet modeling of financial analysis in the computer lab. This includes training on how to work effectively with a spreadsheet to resolve hospitality financial problems and generate financial statements and budgets, which are all addressed in the coursework. This change was necessitated because of the hospitality industry's demand for financial competencies among hospitality graduates. There was a dramatic improvement in the managerial accounting and financial competencies of the students within the first semester of the course innovation. The following comments are just a few of the students' remarks:

- "This is one of the few times I've done a project that took what we learned, made it practical, and showed us how to use the skills in the real world."
- "I enjoyed how it was hands-on learning on a computer almost every day. The lessons that were taught on Excel will definitely benefit my future management positions."
- "I underestimated the value that his (Dr. Ogbeide's) class was going to have on me. I have learned a lot from this class and have even learned a great deal about how to use Excel spreadsheet and figure out the finances of my hotel or restaurant."
- "Without this class I feel like I would not be prepared to go into any industry and be secure with myself and the way I would run the business."

A spreadsheet is the standard tool that hospitality management professionals (including other business professionals) use to analyze quantitative problems, and to financially analyze and manage financial statements. Many computer software companies are now using these spreadsheet programs to build models that are applicable to the hospitality industry and other businesses around the globe. Today, many people worldwide are using these spreadsheet programs to make decisions both at home and at their daily business centers. Hence, the importance of incorporating the spreadsheet-modeling approach to the financial analysis textbook cannot be over enumerated. This addition will simultaneously develop students' ability to utilize the standard tool of today's business world (spreadsheet) and enhance their skills in financial decision making.

The spreadsheet-modeling approach will also capture hospitality students' interests and add new value to their careers, as they will see how it can be applied in everyday hospitality departments and in the business world, in general. This textbook provides concise information needed to enhance the users' knowledge in hospitality operations, revenue management, cost control, and the use of spreadsheets for developing financial statements and solving other quantitative problems. Prior experience in the use of Excel software is certainly valuable but should not be a requirement for using this textbook.

Intended Audiences

Instructors will find this textbook concise but relevant enough to address numerous accounting and financial concepts that are critical to the hospitality industry. The step-by-step spreadsheet-modeling examples provide the instructors an opportunity to use this textbook for an online course dealing with some of the accounting and financial competencies covered here. This book can be used as a required book or recommended to complement other accounting and/or financial textbooks.

Students will find the innovations in this textbook clear and simple enough for better understanding of the accounting and financial terms and concepts covered in the course. The step-by-step spreadsheet-modeling examples provide the students, as well as future managers and mangers, the ability to develop financial statements without the usual complexities and confusion that enfold most managers—other than accountants.

Hospitality professionals will find this textbook useful for addressing numerous operational issues in various organizations. Hence, any manager or owner of a hospitality business can use this textbook to enhance her or his knowledge in hospitality management especially as it relates to financial decision making.

Features

Each chapter includes the following:

- Concise learning objectives.
- Focuses on the necessary facts about the subject matter.
- Definitions of accounting and financial terms.
- Formulas and concepts you should know as a section in each chapter. (This section lists all the formulas and concepts regarding each chapter, which are also useful for solving the examples and the scenario questions.)
- Examples with the step-by-step spreadsheet-modeling approach used to solve the problem.
- Review questions and answers.

About the Author

Dr. Godwin-Charles Ogbeide (PhD, MBA) is a faculty member in the Department of Food, Human Nutrition, and Hospitality Management at the University of Arkansas at Fayetteville. He is an active member of the Professional Convention Management Association (PCMA) and the International Council on Hotel, Restaurant, and Institutional Education (I-CHRIE).

Dr. Ogbeide has developed many courses in hospitality management. Some of the courses he helped develop include Introduction to Hospitality Management; Hotel Operations Management; Food, Beverage, and Labor Cost Management; Food Systems Management; Design and Layout of Foodservice Facility; Front Office Revenue Management; Meetings, Events, and Conventions Management; and Hospitality Operations with Financial Analysis.

Dr. Ogbeide received his MS, and PhD degrees with emphasis in Hospitality Management and Leadership Development from the University of Missouri–Columbia. He also has an MBA with more than twenty-five years of experience in the hospitality industry. He is an advocate and provider of real life, "hands-on" experience that is needed in the hospitality and tourism industries. Dr. Ogbeide is a winner of many awards including "innovation" awards.

Dedication

This book is dedicated to my parents, Mr. Sylvester Ogbeide and Mrs. Esther Ogbeide. Dad, your leadership skills and dedication to community service have inspired me to be doing the same. Mom, your logistic and financial skills and business acumen contributed to who I am today. Thanks to both of you for sharing many experiences with me, supporting my education, and for providing me with real-life, hands-on business experience. I hope this book provides all the users with the common financial analysis, revenue management, and cost-control skills needed to be successful in their business ventures.

Acknowledgments

I would like to acknowledge my wife, Bukola Ogbeide, for her relentless support on this project and for the outstanding love and care she provided the Ogbeide's family household throughout the duration of this project. I also wish to thank each of my children—Enosa, Oti, Osas, and Osi—for your continuous motivation and encouragement to finish this project. You are the best family anyone could ask for. You are super.

I would also like to acknowledge Leanna Potts, my office assistant and everyone at University Readers/Cognella who worked very hard to ensure that this project is completed. A distinctive thank you goes to Becky Smith, Sarah Wheeler, Jess Busch, Chelsey Rogers, and everyone at University Readers/Cognella who have contributed in one way or another to the completion of this project. You are all splendid.

CHAPTER ONE

Introduction to Financial Analysis and Spreadsheet Modeling

Learning Objectives

After studying this chapter, you should be able to:

1. Describe financial analysis.
2. Describe the spreadsheet-modeling approach to financial analysis.
3. Understand the use of numbers in business.
4. Understand how to determine financial performance.
5. Use some basic financial and accounting formulae.
6. Demonstrate the use of spreadsheet modeling in solving some basic financial and accounting problems.

Financial Analysis

Financial analysis seems like a complex and complicated subject. But anybody in business who intends to be successful, including in the hospitality industry, needs to know how to analyze financial documents. If you want to maximize your profit, you need to be able to read and understand your financial statements in order to make appropriate changes that will lead to profit maximization. Similarly, hospitality managers need to able to read, analyze, and understand their establishments' financial statements if they wish to be highly successful in their careers. This chapter presents some essential concepts about financial analysis and spreadsheet modeling. **Financial analysis** is the assessment of a business's monetary affairs, financial statements, budgets, and other finance-related reports for decision-making purposes.

> "I finally know what distinguishes man from the other beasts: financial worries."
>
> *Jules Renard (1864–1910)*
>
> *French writer*

Spreadsheet Modeling

Spreadsheets are common tools that business pros use to analyze financial statements. Today, millions of people, including non-business pros, use spreadsheets for many purposes including financial decision making. **Spreadsheet modeling** of financial statements provides a simplified way to use Microsoft Excel or any other spreadsheet to design and analyze financial statements. Although other spreadsheet software can be used for financial statements, the spreadsheet-modeling approach in this book is based on Microsoft Excel. Prior knowledge and experience with Excel spreadsheet will surely be advantageous, but it is not a requirement for using this text. This text is designed with step-by-step directions and well-defined screenshot examples for easy understanding. One of the major advantages of spreadsheet modeling is that it makes financial analysis and the calculation of financial variables easier and faster.

The Use of Numbers

Financial analysis requires the use of numbers. **Numbers** are figures used to measure quantities, amounts, or statistical facts. In business, numbers are also used to measure the financial performance of an organization. It can be used to indicate the condition of the business to managers and other stakeholders. It can also be used to reveal if the business is:

- Making a profit or producing a loss
- Financially strong or weak (stable, solvent, or liquid)
- Producing at a high or low capacity via specific measures

Numbers in different forms can be used by managers for planning and decision making. This can be in the form of inventory cost control, budgeting, revenue forecast, labor cost control, etc. Financial statements are based on numbers. The three major financial statements used in business, including the hospitality industry, are the income statement (P&L statement), balance sheet, and cash flow statement. All are used to measure the financial performance of business organizations.

Financial Reports and Numbers

Financial reports are based on the reading and understanding of numbers. The numbers, however, are meaningless unless they are used to measure a specific venture. The venture could be the organization's goal or the basic comparison of budgets and other financial reports. Some of the common financial reports that are based on the comparison of numbers of one specific period to another include: (1) financial statements, (2) forecasts, and (3) budgets. These reports are usually compared from one period (month, quarter, or year) to another to determine whether the period is worse or better than the previous period. Such comparisons help management in determining if the organization is:

- Advancing in the right direction as planned.
- Reaching, exceeding, or not reaching its planned goals.
- Identifying daily, weekly, or monthly trends in operations for potential adjustments as needed.

Financial Performance and Profitability

The objective measure of business success is the business entity's financial performance, and the common indicator of a business's positive financial performance is profitability. This does not undermine the importance of customers' and employees' satisfaction. In fact, your business financial performance will be greatly enhanced if your customers and employees are satisfied. Bearing the above in mind, it is clear that profit maximization is one of the major objectives of business owners. The words **profit, income,** and **earnings** are the same and can be used interchangeably. Some of the profit measures commonly used in business include gross profit, operating profit, net profit, and net profit after tax.

Gross Profit: Equals total sales (revenue) minus the cost of goods sold (COGS). It is the first tier of profit in an income statement. It is basically the profit generated by the business without the operating costs and taxes.

Net Profit Before Tax: Equals total sales (revenue) minus the cost of goods sold (COGS) and all other operating expenses except taxes. It is also known as earnings before tax, net income before tax, pretax income, or net operating income before taxes.

Net Profit After Tax: Equals total sales (revenue) minus the cost of goods sold (COGS) and all other operating expenses and taxes. It is also known as earnings after tax, net income after tax, or net income.

To calculate profit, the management staff must understand basic arithmetic. Some of the most common formulas in financial analysis and accounting require the mere understanding of addition, subtraction, multiplication, and division. See examples of some common formulas below:

Formulas

1.1. Gross Profit = Revenue − COGS

1.2. Net Profit Before Tax (NPBT) = Revenue − (COGS + All Other Expenses)

1.3. Net Profit After Tax (NPAT) = NPBT − (NPBT × Tax Rate)

1.4. Revenue = Average Customer Expenditure (ACE) × Volume (# of customers served)

1.5. Revenue = Average Daily Rate (ADR) × Volume (# of rooms sold)

1.6. $\text{ADR} = \dfrac{\text{Total Room Revenue}}{\text{Total \# of Rooms Sold}}$

1.7. $\text{RevPAR} = \dfrac{\text{Total Room Revenue}}{\text{Total \# of Rooms Available}}$

1.8. Total Rooms Sold = Occupancy Rate × Total # of Rooms Available

---

Revenue in the above formulas refers to the total sales. The revenue formula in the fourth formula is used mostly for restaurants, while the fifth formula's revenue is used mostly in the lodging (motel and hotel) industries. The importance of these formulas at this point is that they are each basic arithmetic formulas. To use any of the above formulas to calculate the variable they represent, we need to know the other two variables and apply the proper arithmetic formula. Now that we are familiar with some basic arithmetic formulas and their uses, let us try some examples.

Spreadsheet-Modeling Approach to Solving Examples 1.1–1.4

Obviously, a manager with a good handle on how to use a calculator and a great understanding of the appropriate formulas to use can solve Examples 1.1–1.4 above. But what if the manager made a mistake and keyed in the wrong figures while using the calculator? The manager would then have to restart the calculation. Hence, that would make the calculation tedious and take a longer time to finish. This is precisely why a spreadsheet-modeling approach to financial analysis cannot be overlooked.

Spreadsheet Design Guiding Principles

1. **Organize the data using the given variables:** It is very critical to arrange the variables in a visually pleasing manner (i.e., series of each variable in one column or row) for easy understanding and location of the variables. A good organization of the variable will also enhance the credibility and auditability of the spreadsheet model.
2. **Incorporate cells in your formulas:** A design that incorporates cells in formulas that can be copied to do a series of calculations is more understandable and less prone to mistakes than the alternatives. Once the first formula is done correctly, it can be copied to solve the other series of calculations. In addition, if there is a mistake in data entering, once the mistake is corrected the calculations would be automatically corrected.
3. **Keep total at the end of a column or row:** It is very common for spreadsheet users to expect the number at the end of a column or row to be the total of the calculation of the data in that column or row. Numbers that do not represent the total of a column or row should be clearly labeled to prevent misinterpretation of the column or row.
4. **Data entry design:** It is common for data entry in the spreadsheet to be from top to bottom and left to right. This should be considered when designing a spreadsheet to enhance the consistency, readability, and auditability of the spreadsheet model.
5. **Distinguish changeable columns or rows:** Use shading, borders, and/or colors to distinguish changeable columns or rows of variables. This makes it easy to identify and modify the columns or rows in case of a mistake.
6. **Create text boxes with cell notes:** Use text boxes and cell notes to keep a record of how each decision variable in the spreadsheet model was calculated. This will enhance the understanding and auditability of the spreadsheet model.
7. **The use of equal sign (=):** When starting a calculation in the Excel spreadsheet, the first thing to type into the "cell" that instructs Excel to calculate is the equal sign (=).

EXAMPLE 1.1:

Question: If the average customer expenditure of a Charley's Restaurant is $21.50/day for a year, what is the annual revenue of the restaurant if Average Customer Count = 250/day for the year?

ANSWER

Formula: Revenue = Average Customer Expenditure (ACE) × Volume (# of customers served)
Variables Needed: ACE = $21.50; Volume = 250/day, but the question is asking for the annual (year) revenue. Hence, Volume = 250 × 365 (days in a year) = 91,250
Therefore, Annual Revenue = $21.50 × 91,250 = **$1,961,875**

EXAMPLE 1.2:

Question: Following up with Example 1.1, what is the gross profit of Charley's Restaurant if its cost of goods sold (COGS) is $500,000 and all other expenses are $1 million per year?

ANSWER

Formula: Gross Profit = Revenue − COGS
Variables Needed: Revenue = $1,961,875; COGS = $500,000
Therefore, Gross Profit = $1,961,875 − $500,000 = **$1,461,875**

EXAMPLE 1.3:

Question: Following up with Example 1.1, what is the net profit before tax (NPBT) of Charley's Restaurant if its cost of goods sold (COGS) is $500,000 and all other expenses are $1 million per year?

ANSWER

Formula: Net Profit Before Tax (NPBT) = Revenue − (COGS + All Other Expenses)
Variables Needed: Revenue = $1,961,875; COGS = $500,000; all other expenses = $1,000,000
Therefore, NPBT = $1,961,875 − ($500,000 + $1,000,000) = **$461,875**

EXAMPLE 1.4:

Question: Following up with Example 1.3, what is the net profit after tax (NPAT) of Charley's Restaurant if its appropriate tax rate is 35 percent?

ANSWER

Formula: Net Profit After Tax (NPAT) = NPBT − (NPBT × Tax Rate)
Variables Needed: NPBT = $461,875; Tax Rate = 35%
Therefore, NPBT = $461,875 − ($461,875 × 35%)
$$= \$461,875 - \$161,656.25$$
$$= \underline{\$300,218.75}$$

STEP-BY-STEP, HANDS-ON APPROACH TO EXAMPLES 1.1–1.4

1. In your Excel spreadsheet, label cells B1, C1, and D1 as *Variable*, *Day*, and *Annual*, respectively.
2. Identify your given variables (*ACE* and *Volume*) and label them in B2 and B3, respectively.
3. Insert the value of the given variable under the appropriate label. ACE value is $21.50 per day. Hence, it is inserted under the label *Day*. Because the ACE will be the same per year, it is also inserted under *Annual*. Similarly, volume is 250 per day. Hence, it is inserted under *Day*; however, volume for the year is 91,250 (C3 * 365 [days in a year]), which you should calculate in cell D3.
4. Identify the question (annual revenue) and label it under *Variable* as in B4 with a question mark in D4.
5. You don't have to insert the *formula* as labeled in B5 under *Variable*, as inserted in D5, because your computations will always keep your formulas. But it is helpful for ensuring that your computation is done as intended.
6. To solve Example 1.1, compute the annual revenue as labeled in B6 by typing the following in D6: =D2 * D3. If your arrangement is correct the value should show as **$1,961,875**.
7. To solve Example 1.2, gross profit as labeled in B8 with a question mark in D8. We need to include the additional given variables (*COGS* and *All Other Expenses*) and label them as in B9 and B10, respectively.
8. Insert the value of the given variable under the appropriate label. COGS value is $500,000 per year. Hence, it is inserted under the label *Annual* as in D9. Because All Other Expenses is also per year, it too is inserted under *Annual* as in D10.
9. The formula for gross profit is equal to revenue minus cost of goods sold. Hence, B8 = D6 – D9 as inserted in D11.
10. Compute gross profit as labeled in B12 by typing the following in D12: =D6 – D9. If your arrangement is correct the value should show as **$1,461,875**.
11. To solve Example 1.3, net profit before tax (NPBT) as labeled in B14 with a question mark in D14.
12. The formula for NPBT is equal to revenue minus the addition of COGS and All Other Expenses. Hence, B14 = D6 – (D9 + D10) as inserted in D15.
13. Compute NPBT as labeled in B16 by typing the following in D16: =D6 – (D9 + D10). If your arrangement is correct the value should show as **$461,875**.
14. To solve Example 1.4, net profit after tax (NPAT) as labeled in B18 with a question mark in D18.
15. Insert the value of the given variable under the appropriate label. Tax rate value is 35 percent all year round. Hence, it is inserted under the label *Annual* as in D19.
16. The formula for NPAT is equal to NPBT minus the solution of NPBT multiplied by the tax rate, B18 = D16 – (D16 * D19) as inserted in D20.
17. Compute NPAT as labeled in B21 by typing the following in D21: =D16 – (D16 * D19). If your arrangement is correct the value should be **$300,218.75**.

Exhibit 1.1: Spreadsheet-Modeling Approach to Examples 1.1–1.4

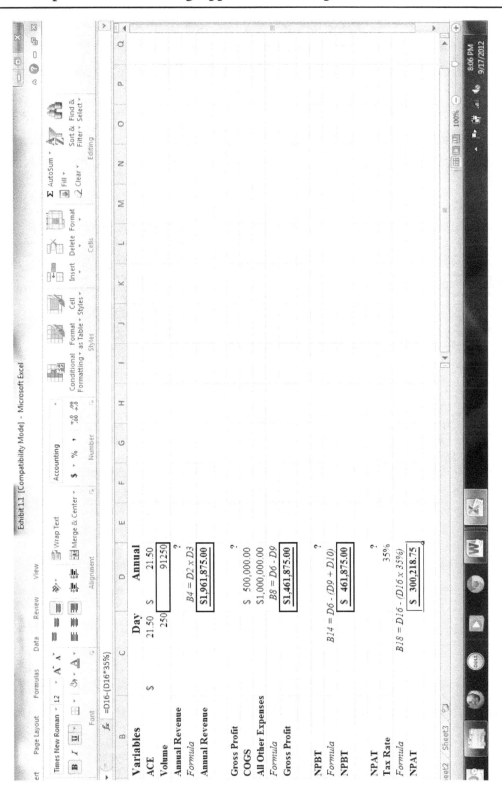

The above examples and spreadsheet model represent a food service transaction and the computation of its revenue, net profit before tax, and net profit after tax. The next example will explain the computation of lodging industry (motel, hotel, and resort) revenue. It is very critical to understand how revenue and other variables needed for the computation of revenue in the lodging industry are measured. Knowing and understanding the formulas is a fundamental key to solving and analyzing lodging industry financial and accounting problems.

EXAMPLE 1.5:

Question: What is the room revenue of a hotel if 80 percent of its 300 available rooms were sold at an ADR of $100?

ANSWER

Formula: Revenue = Average Daily Rate (ADR) × Volume (Total # of Rooms Sold)

Variables Needed: ADR = $100; Volume = Total # of Rooms Sold, which is not given. Hence, we have to compute the volume before we can apply the formula.

Total # of Rooms Sold = Occupancy Rate × Total # of Rooms Available

$$= 80\% \times 300$$
$$= 240$$

Therefore, Revenue = ADR × Volume (Total # of Rooms Available)

$$= \$100 \times 240$$
$$= \underline{\$24,000}$$

Spreadsheet-Modeling Approach to Solving Example 1.5

Again, a manager with a good handle on how to use a calculator and a great understanding of the appropriate formulas to use can solve Example 1.5 above. And again, if the manager should make a mistake in entering the figures he would then have to restart the computation. This is one of the major reasons a spreadsheet-modeling approach to financial analysis cannot be ignored.

STEP-BY-STEP, HANDS-ON APPROACH TO EXAMPLE 1.5

1. In your Excel spreadsheet label B1 and C1 as *Variable* and *Period*, respectively.
2. Identify your given variables (*Occupancy rate*, *Available room*, and *ADR*) and label them as in B2, B3, and B4, respectively.
3. Insert the value of the given variable under the appropriate label. Occupancy rate value is 80 percent per the period in question. Hence, it is inserted under the label *Period*. Similarly, available room and ADR values are also inserted under *Period*. Hence, they are all inserted under *Period* as in C2, C3, and C4, respectively.
4. The formula for rooms' revenue is equal to the average daily rate multiplied by volume (total # of rooms sold). Hence, B5 = C4 × Volume (Total # of Rooms Sold).
5. Since the total # of rooms sold is not given, it needs to be computed. The formula for total # of rooms sold is equal to occupancy rate multiplied by total # of rooms available (C2 × C3) as indicated in B8.
6. *Compute the Total # of Rooms Sold* as labeled in B9 by typing the following in C9: = C2 * C3. If your arrangement is correct the value should be **240**.
7. To solve Example 1.5 for *Revenue* as labeled in B11, type the following in C11: = C4 * C9. If your arrangement is correct the value should be **$24,000**.

Exhibit 1.2: Spreadsheet-Modeling Approach to Example 1.5

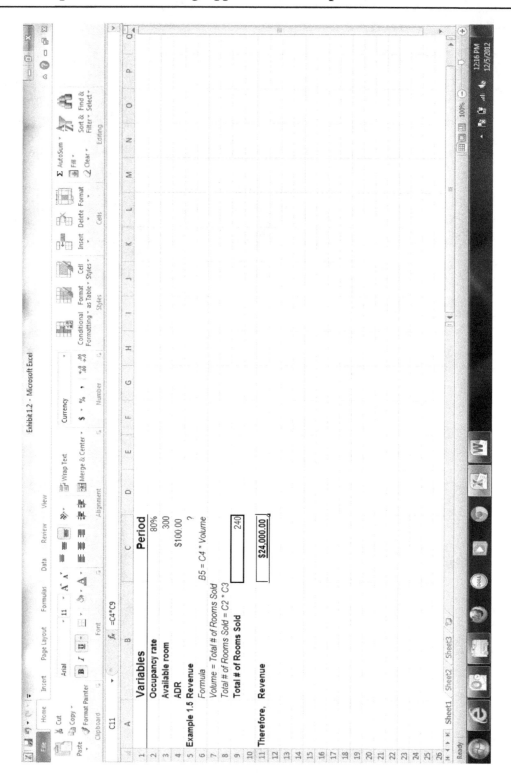

The spreadsheet shows the following content:

	A	B	C
1		Variables	**Period**
2		Occupancy rate	80%
3		Available room	300
4		ADR	$100.00
5		Example 1.5 Revenue	?
6		Formula	B5 = C4 * Volume
7		Volume = Total # of Rooms Sold	
8		Total # of Rooms Sold = C2 * C3	
9		Total # of Rooms Sold	240
10			
11		**Therefore, Revenue**	$24,000.00

Pro Forma Earnings Statement

Most organizations depend on their past performances to predict future performances or budgets. New organizations, however, have no past performance to rely on for future performance, and therefore rely on a critically designed pro forma earnings statement that is based on the economic conditions and other demand and supply factors in the area where the organization is located. The **pro forma earnings statement** is a projected earnings statement based on rational assumptions, which is usually used in support of a business plan or proposal. The pro forma earnings statement is basically an estimate of how the organization will perform in the first year of business. In some cases when a business loan is needed, the bank could request for up to three to five years of pro forma earnings statements. The pro forma earnings statement after the first year of business is then used to predict future performance including cash flow statements, which are helpful in determining the ability to repay the loan and/or loan repayment plan.

Difference in Performance

The importance of management's ability to notice the differences in performance from one period to another cannot be overly enumerated. Managers should be able to read and understand numbers to detect changes in performance and identify sources and courses of changes. A good financial analysis should be able to indicate whether the changes are associated with any of the following variables: revenue, customer count or volume, price or rate, cost of sales, salaries and wages, benefits, expenses, etc. Then, an effective manager should be able to use the results of the financial analysis to enhance the organization's performance.

"Successful entrepreneurs judge correctly the need for change, then do something about it."
James Edward, Lord Hanson (1922–2004)
British business executive and entrepreneur

Assessing Change in Performance

How will you know whether a change is good or bad? How will you know whether you are meeting the objectives of your departments? Some of the common ways in accounting and finance are to assess the amount in units (e.g., dollars) or the performance percentage in comparison to the stated objectives.

When assessing performance change based on the amount generated, management must be very careful about what it is trying to communicate to the shareholders or business owners. For example, one of the objectives of management is to increase the average revenue above $100,000 per month. The average revenue of $105,000 per month indicates an increase of $5,000 in the average revenue per month. Hence, management accomplished the objective.

But when assessing performance change based on percentage, you need to be able to calculate and understand the meaning of the percentage change calculated. For example, one of your objectives is to increase revenue by 5 percent. The previous year's revenue was $1.2

million. A 5 percent increase in revenue is $60,000 ($1.2 million * 5 percent), plus last year's revenue ($1.2 million) equals $1,260,000. Hence, you need to make $1,260,000 in revenue to reach your objective of a 5 percent increase in revenue for the following year. If at the end of the year your total revenue is $1,250,000, even though you increased the revenue by $50,000 ($1,250,000 – $1,200,000), you still did not reach your stated objective. This is one of the reasons an effective manager has to be good with financial analysis and be aware of historical data (past performances), economic conditions, and other demand and supply factors in the area where the organization is located when making projections.

"It is an immutable law in business that words are words, explanations are explanations, promises are promises—but only performance is reality."
Harold S. Geneen (1910–1997)
US telecommunications entrepreneur and CEO of ITT

Percentage is one of the most common descriptive statistics used for assessing relationships or change in performance. Percentages are ratios or proportions of something in relation to the whole thing. For example, we have ten students in a class. If four of the ten students are boys, the percentage of boys in that class is 40 percent (4/10 * 100). Similarly, the percentage of girls in that class is 60 percent (6/10 * 100). The percentage difference between girls and boys is 20 percent (60 – 40) or ([6 – 4]/10 *100).

Another example of the use of percentage is in the assessment of one of the variables in the P&L in relation to the total revenue. Twenty-eight percent labor cost means that for every dollar generated in revenue by that organization, twenty-eight cents is spent on employees' labor cost used to generate the revenue. Similarly, 5 percent marketing cost means that for every dollar generated in revenue by that organization, five cents is spent on marketing cost used to generate the revenue.

Formulas

1.9. Employees' Labor Cost Percentage $= \dfrac{\text{Employees' Salaries + Wages in Dollars}}{\text{Associated Total Revenue in Dollars}}$

1.10. Marketing Cost Percentage $= \dfrac{\text{Marketing Cost in Dollars}}{\text{Associated Total Revenue in Dollars}}$

Accounting and Financial Terminology

Balance sheet *is a financial report that shows the net worth of an organization in the form of assets, liabilities, and owners' equity at a specific point in time.*

Cash flow statement *is a financial report that shows how much cash is generated, used, and retained by an organization in a specific period.*

Financial analysis *is the assessment of a business's monetary affairs, financial statements, budgets, and other finance-related reports for decision-making purposes.*

Income statement *is a financial report that shows the revenue, expenses, and profit or loss of an organization for a specified time period (e.g., a month, quarter, or year). The income statement is also known as a profit and loss (P&L) statement, earnings statement, or operating statement.*

Numbers *are figures used to measure quantities, amounts, or statistical facts. In business, numbers are also used to measure financial performance of an organization.*

Pro forma earnings statement *is a projected earnings statement based on rational assumptions, which is usually used in support of a business plan or proposal.*

Spreadsheet modeling *of financial statements provides a simplified way to use Microsoft Excel or any other spreadsheet to design and analyze financial statements.*

Summary

Financial analysis is the assessment of businesses monetary affairs, financial statements, budgets, and other finance-related reports for decision-making purposes. Hospitality managers need to be able to read, analyze, and understand their establishments' financial statements to realize highly successful careers.

Spreadsheet modeling of financial statements provides a simplified way to use Microsoft Excel or any other spreadsheet to create and analyze financial statements. One of the major advantages of spreadsheet modeling is that it makes financial analysis and the calculation of financial variables easier and faster.

Financial analysis requires the use of numbers. Financial statements are based on numbers, and numbers in different forms can be used by managers for planning and decision making. Financial reports are based on the reading and understanding of numbers. Some of the more common financial reports that are based on the comparison of numbers of one specific period to another include: (1) financial statements, (2) forecasts, and (3) budgets.

Profit maximization is one of the major objectives of business owners. The words *profit*, *income*, and *earnings* are the same and can be used interchangeably.

Keywords and Concepts

Average Daily Rate (ADR)	Income Statement
Balance Sheet	Net Profit After Tax
Cash Flow Statement	Net Profit Before Tax
Cost of Goods Sold	Numbers
Cost Percentage	Occupancy Rate
Employees Labor Cost Percentage	Pro Forma Earnings Statement
Financial Analysis	Revenue
Financial Report	Revenue Per Available Room (RevPAR)
Gross Profit	Spreadsheet Modeling

Review Questions

1. What is the occupancy percentage of a hotel with 400 rooms available for sale that sold 300 rooms last night, with a total rooms' revenue of $33,000?

2. What is the room revenue of a hotel, with 80 percent of its 400 rooms sold, at an ADR of $100?

3. What is the revenue per available room of a hotel, with 80 percent of its 400 rooms sold, at an ADR of $100?

4. The average customer expenditure (ACE) of Charley's Restaurant is $21/day with an average customer count of 250/day for the year. Charley's Restaurant's cost of goods sold (COGS) is $600,000 and all other expenses are $900,000 per year? Answer the following questions:
   a. What is the annual revenue of Charley's Restaurant?
   b. What is the gross profit of Charley's Restaurant?
   c. What is the net profit before tax (NPBT) of Charley's Restaurant?
   d. What is Charley's Restaurant's net profit after tax (NPAT) if its appropriate tax rate is 35 percent?

5. What is the profit of Charley's Restaurant if all its expenses are $1.5 million per year, with an average customer expenditure of $21/day and an average customer count of 250/day for the year?

6. What is the labor cost percentage of Charley's Restaurant if its payroll and related expenses (employees' salaries + wages in dollars) are $498,225 per year, with an average customer expenditure of $21/day and an average customer count of 250/day for the year?

7. What is the marketing cost of Charley's Restaurant if all its marketing expenses are $76,650 per year, with an average customer expenditure of $21/day and an average customer count of 250/day for the year?

8. Last year a restaurant did monthly sales of $95,000. This year the restaurant increased that by $5,000—that is, to $100,000. But the budget was $110,000, which means the

restaurant missed the budget by $10,000. Based on that information, answer the following questions:

a. Is this good or bad? Why?
b. By what percentage was the revenue supposed to increase?
c. By what percentage was the revenue increase?
d. By what percentage did the restaurant miss the budget?
e. If the entire $100,000 in monthly sales was from room's revenue, what were the number of rooms sold if ADR was $80?

CHAPTER TWO

Accounting Operations in the Hospitality Industry

Learning Objectives

After studying this chapter, you should be able to:

1. Describe accounting concepts.
2. Describe different types of accounting.
3. Understand the process of internal control and auditing of annual reports.
4. Describe the uses and users of accounting/financial reports.
5. Understand and apply the generally accepted accounting principle (GAAP).
6. Describe income statement, balance sheet, and cash flow statement.

What is Accounting

Accounting is basically a system for compiling and reporting an organization's monetary information for making economic decisions. The monetary information is used for making appropriate decisions by the organization's management, business owners, creditors, government, board of directors, employees, investors, banks, and others interested in the organization's business. This chapter focuses on the basic accounting concepts and application of those concepts in the hospitality industry.

Key Hospitality Accounting Information

Financial Accounting: Refers to accounting information that focuses on reporting an organization's transactions, performance, and financial position. Financial accounting includes the periodic reporting of information to parties outside the organization. Some examples of financial accounting reports include income statement, balance sheet, and cash flow statement.

Managerial Accounting: Refers to accounting information based on the identification, analysis, and interpretation of historical and/or projected financial data, which are used by the management for making daily and future operational plans. Unlike financial accounting that mainly provides information to people outside the organization, managerial accounting information is mainly used to help managers within the organization make daily and future operational decisions.

Cost Accounting: Refers to a subdivision of managerial accounting that focuses on cost control. It includes the identification, analysis, and interpretation of cost data, which are used by the management for making daily and future operational plans.

Accounting System

It is very important for business organizations to have an accounting system for creating financial statements, reports to managers, bills to customers, income tax, and other types of accounting and financial information. An **accounting system** includes the procedures, devices, personnel, and other records used by an organization to develop accounting information and report the information to decision makers. Accounting systems in the hospitality industry often make use of computers, point of sale (POS), property management systems (PMS), and other electronic systems and well-organized handwritten records.

Internal Control and Auditing Processes

Internal control is a way to assure management that the accounting information reported via the accounting system is correct and reliable. Some examples of hospitality internal control procedures include the use of serial numbers on issued checks, the inscription of transaction date and time on receipts, daily monitoring of the inventory, and keeping records of changes to guest accounts via provided documents. Internal control measures basically include all the possible means used by organizations to prevent theft, waste, fraud, and errors. A good internal control measure will enhance the reliability of the accounting records and ensure that the organization operates as planned. The importance of internal control to stakeholders cannot be overly enumerated. The stakeholders need to be assured that the financial statements provided by the management indicate a complete and reliable financial condition of the organization. In most cases, this assurance is provided by an audit of the organization's accounting records.

Audit: Refers to an important part of accounting that focuses on an independent review and verification of accounting records. Auditing is a critical part of hospitality daily operations. An effective hospitality manager should have a system of making sure the organization's accounting system adheres to the following:

- All credits and debits from the previous day are posted.
- Verify the financial reports for accuracy.
- Validate changes to guest accounts via provided documents or other evidence.
- Daily account is accurate before the beginning of a new day.

"Nothing is more central to an organization's effectiveness than its ability to transmit accurate, relevant, understandable information among its members."

Saul W. Gellerman
US psychologist and writer

In the hotel industry, the **night auditor** plays a major role in ensuring that the daily account is accurate before the beginning of a new business day. The night auditor's role is one of the most significant roles in the hotel industry because of the responsibilities and discipline needed to do the job, coupled with the fact that the audit is usually done in the early morning hours (between 12 and 5 a.m.). The time varies by several hours because it depends on the organization's prescribed audit time, and how busy the organization is prior to the night audit. In the restaurant and other hospitality industries, management should create a system of internal control or seek the services of experts such as a certified public accountant (CPA). With the advent of POS systems, management can easily review guest checks and monitor inventory at anytime during their shift. See Exhibit 2.1 for the process of auditing financial statements and annual reports by an independent reviewer.

The accurate annual report provided to the public in Exhibit 2.1 includes the audited financial statements, notes about the financial statements, auditor's report, management's discussion of results, and any other information that could help the stakeholders make appropriate decisions about their interest in the organization.

Exhibit 2.1: The Process of Auditing Financial Statements and Annual Reports

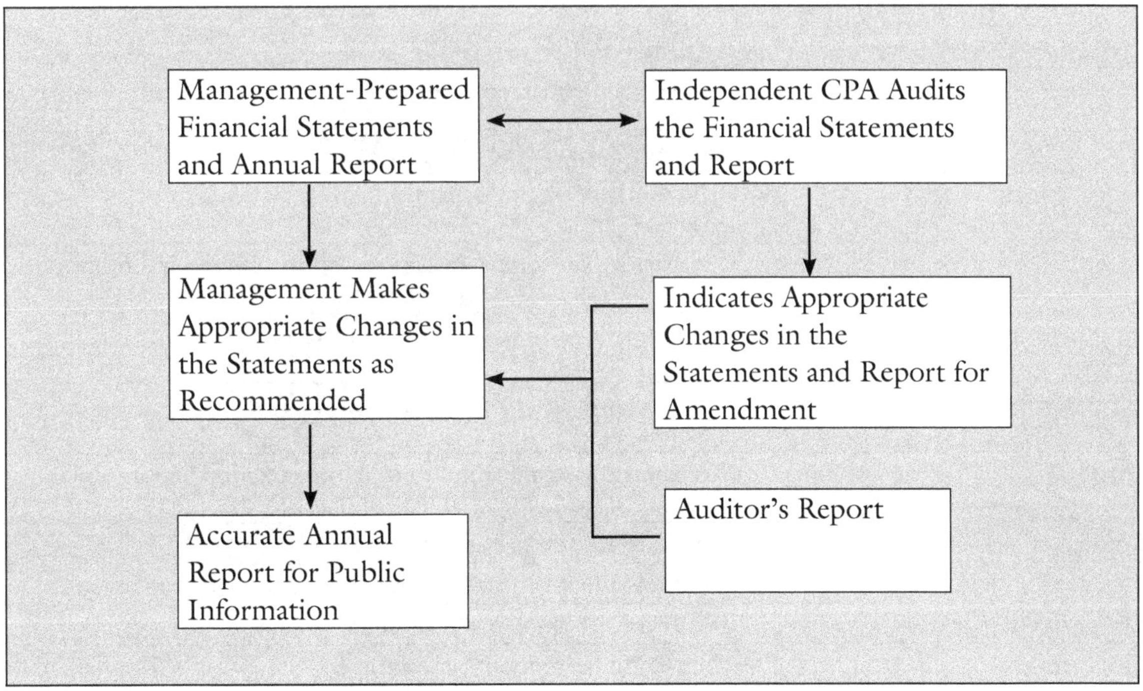

Users of Annual Report

The annual reports are used by stakeholders inside and outside of the organization. Inside the organization, management uses the annual report to evaluate past performance, make new plans, and achieve internal control.

Outside the organization, many stakeholders use the annual report for different reasons. Investors/owners use it to identify and assess investment opportunities and to monitor the condition of their investment. Banks use it to assess credit worthiness, whether to extend loans to organizations and how much to lend. Investment advisors use it predict future performances of the organization and the economy. Clients use it assess the sustainability of the organization and its ability to service its products. Employees use it to assess the employer's ability to pay them. Students use it for learning about business. The general public uses it to know the impact of the organization on the economy. Government agencies use it to formulate appropriate policies, and competitors use it to plan for competitive advantage. See Exhibit 2.2 for the users of the annual report and the purposes of its use.

Generally Accepted Accounting Principles (GAAP)

Generally accepted accounting principles (GAAP) are the generally accepted rules for financial reporting. These principles provide consistency and the general framework for the preparation of financial statements. For GAAP to work for business organizations, it requires some form of authoritative support and enforcement, and must be adopted and used by all the business organizations.

Exhibit 2.2: Users of Annual Report

Users of Annual Report	Purpose of Use
Management	To evaluate past performance, make new plans, and achieve internal control.
Investors/Owners	To identify and assess investment opportunities and to monitor the condition of their investment.
Banks (Creditors)	To decide whether to extend loans to organizations and how much to lend.
Investment Advisors	To predict future performances of the organization and the economy.
Clients	To assess the sustainability of the organization and its ability to service its products.
Students	For learning about business.
General Public	To know the impact of the organization on the economy.
Government Agencies	To formulate appropriate policies.
Competitors	To plan for competitive advantage.

Selected Accounting Principles

Business Entity Concepts

GAAP require that established financial statements be used to describe the activities of each business organization. Individual or personal accounts or spending should be separated from business accounts or spending. Business accounting and financial activities should be separate from the person or persons who supply the business's assets. Similarly, the financial records of the business and business owner(s) should be separate. The idea behind the business entity principle is that for accounting and record-keeping purposes, the personal activities of the business owner(s) are separate from the affairs of the business entity.

The Fundamental Accounting Equation

The necessary characteristic of every balance sheet (assets and liability statement) is that the total assets equal the total of liabilities plus the owner's equity. This phenomenon is one fundamental reason for calling this statement a balance sheet. The assets should always be equal to the liabilities and owner's equity because it is simply an outlook of one business entity from two points of views. One outlook is from the assets' point of view, which shows what the business entity owns. The second outlook is from the liabilities' and owner's equity, which discloses who supplied the assets or the resources making up the assets, while the owner's equity is the difference between the total assets and the total liabilities. Hence, the total assets of the business entity equal the total resources supplied by creditors plus the claims of the owner(s).

Money as a Unit of Measure

The main purpose for starting a business is to make money. To maintain uniform financial records, it is essential to have a unit of measure. As such, money is the common unit of measure. In regard to this accounting principle, only transactions that can be recorded in monetary terms should be included in an organization's financial records. This principle is not intended to negate other relevant outputs of business such as customers' satisfaction, employees' satisfaction, quality of employees or service, etc. It is very essential as a means to measure the total net worth of the business entity.

"Money turns out to be whatever we agree it to be. It is a collective work of the imagination."
Simon Carr, British journalist
Source: Independent *(London) (January 12, 2009)*

Cost Principle

Cost refers to the amount of money spent on goods or services during a transaction. The cost principle of accounting requires business entities to record the organization's transactions at its original cost at the time of transaction. The importance of this principle is that it provides a simplified way to use the original cost (purchase price) as a confirmable indication of the value of products and services.

Cash Basis of Accounting

The cash basis of accounting is an accounting method that recognizes a transaction at the time of cash inflow or outflow. In other words, this is an accounting system that recognizes revenues and expenses at the time the cash is actually received or paid out. For example, a general service contractor hired by a show organizer secures a contract toward the end of 2012, with a completion in 2012. But the general service contractor won't be paid until 2013. Therefore, the general service contractor's income statements would be misleading if they are based on the cash basis of accounting. The general service contractor's efforts toward the end of 2012 would not be recognized in the company's income statement at the end of 2012 because the cash basis of accounting recognizes revenues and expenses at the time the cash is actually received or paid out.

Accrual Bases of Accounting

The accrual basis of accounting, in contrast with the cash basis of accounting, is an accounting method that recognizes the transaction when the revenues are earned and the expenses are incurred. In other words, this is an accounting system that recognizes revenues and expenses at the time the transaction is completed, even if the income from the transaction is still pending. For example, the general service contractor is hired by a show organizer using the cash basis of accounting as described above. The transaction is completed in 2012, but not paid until 2013. Therefore, unlike the cash basis of accounting, the general service contractor's effort toward the end of 2012 would be recognized in the company's income statement at the end of 2012 because the accrual basis of accounting recognizes the transaction at the time the product or service is provided, even if the income from the transaction is still pending.

Matching Revenues and Expenses

The matching principle of accounting involves matching revenues with all related expenses during the accounting period in which the obligations are incurred. For example, a hotel food service director may purchase food to be sold in one accounting period. According to the matching principle of accounting, the expense in that accounting period is the cost of food sold to earn the revenue that is recorded in that accounting period. Therefore, when the expenses from one period are matched with the revenue from the same period, the resulting difference is the profit or loss for that period.

"It's not how much you earn, it's how much you owe."
Ted Turner (1938–), US founder of Turner Broadcasting Systems and CNN
Source: Speech (1986)

Depreciation

Depreciation is an accounting principle of allocating the cost associated with the purchase of a tangible asset over its estimated useful life. One of the important features of depreciation for accounting purposes is that it specifies how much of the tangible asset's value has been used up (depreciated) over its estimated useful life. Two common methods used for depreciation are the straight-line depreciation method and the accelerated depreciation method. Organizations may use any of the depreciation methods as long as the method used results in a rational and systematic allocation of cost over the estimated useful life of the asset.

The **straight-line depreciation** method recognizes an equal portion of the asset's cost as depreciation expense over the estimated useful life of the asset. The **accelerated depreciation** method recognizes larger amounts of the asset's cost as depreciation expense in the early years and declining amounts in subsequent years over the estimated useful life of the asset. Depreciation is basically used in an effort to balance the expense of an asset to the income that the asset helps to earn for the organization. For example, a company buys a piece of equipment with a useful life of five years for $250,000. During the five-year depreciation period, the organization will expense $50,000 (assuming straight-line depreciation) every accounting year, which should match the money that the equipment makes each year within the five-year period.

Adequate Disclosure

Adequate disclosure is an important accounting principle that requires that all readers of a financial statement have access to pertinent data necessary for the understanding of the organization's financial position. This principle mandates that financial statements and all other information necessary for full understanding of the financial statements be made available to stakeholders. Such information might include unusual issues that could affect the financial statement, the accounting method used, footnotes, etc.

Consistency Principle

The consistency principle mandates that once an accounting method is adopted by an organization, it should be consistently used from one period to another to make financial statements comparable. In the case of a necessary change to the accounting method, the generally accepted accounting principle requires a full disclosure of the change and the impact of the change to the financial statements.

Revenue and Cost Centers in the Hospitality Industry

In terms of financial resources management, hospitality departments can be classified into revenue (sales) and cost (expenses) centers. This classification is based on whether the department generates revenue for the organization or incurs costs to support either the organization or the departments that generate revenue.

Revenue centers in the hospitality industry are operating departments that produce revenues (sales) by providing products and/or services that generate revenue to clients. These departments are referred to as revenue centers because the products and/or services they provide to the clients are paid for, which translate into revenue for the organization. The two most obvious revenue centers in the lodging industry are: (1) the food and beverage department, which generates revenue from the sale of products in restaurants, lounges, room services, catering, banquets, and vending; and (2) the front office department, which generates revenue from the sale of guest rooms. Other examples of revenue centers in the lodging industry include gift shops, spas, telephone service, parking fees, business centers, space rental, and recreation product sales, rentals, and/or services from golf, tennis, etc.

ACCOUNTING AND FINANCIAL TERMINOLOGY

Accelerated depreciation *is a method of depreciation that recognizes larger amounts of the asset's cost as depreciation expense in the early years and declining amounts in subsequent years over the estimated useful life of the asset.*

Accounting *is basically a system for compiling and reporting an organization's monetary information for making economic decisions.*

Accounting system *includes the procedures, devices, personnel, and other records used by an organization to develop accounting information and reporting the information to decision makers.*

Annual report *is a document issued annually to the public to help stakeholders and potential stakeholders evaluate the organization's past performance, and make plans and decisions about their stake in the organization.*

Auditing *is an independent review and verification of accounting records.*

Cost accounting *is a subdivision of managerial accounting that focuses on cost control.*

Cost or expense centers *in the hospitality industry are the staff departments that support the operating departments that generate sales.*

Depreciation *is an accounting principle of allocating the cost associated with the purchase of a tangible asset over its estimated useful life.*

Financial accounting *focuses on reporting an organization's transaction, performance, and financial position to parties outside the organization.*

Generally accepted accounting principles *are accounting concepts, standard of measurements, and standard of presentation mandated to be used in financial statements.*

Internal control *is a way to assure management that the accounting information that is reported via the accounting system is correct and reliable.*

> **Managerial accounting** *is the identification, analysis, and interpretation of historical and/ or projected financial data used to assist management in making daily and future operational plans.*
>
> **Revenue centers** *in the hospitality industry are operating departments that produce revenues (sales) by providing products and/or services that generate revenue to clients.*
>
> **Straight-line depreciation** *is a depreciating method that recognizes an equal portion of the asset's cost as depreciation expense over the estimated useful life of the asset.*

Cost or expense centers in the hospitality industry are the staff departments that support the operating departments that generate sales. These departments are referred to as cost centers because their budgets only include expenses without any source of direct revenue. Examples of cost centers include sales and marketing, human resources, engineering and maintenance, security, and accounting departments.

Summary

Accounting is a system for compiling and reporting an organization's monetary information for making economic decisions. Financial accounting focuses on reporting an organization's transaction, performance, and financial position. Managerial accounting is based on the identification, analysis, and interpretation of historical and/or projected financial data, which are used by management for making daily and future operational plans. Cost accounting is a subdivision of managerial accounting, which focuses on cost control.

Internal control is a way to assure management and other stakeholders that the accounting information that is reported via the accounting system is correct and reliable. The audit is used to assure all the stakeholders that the financial statements provided by management indicate a complete and reliable financial condition of the organization.

The financial statements and annual report audited by an independent reviewer are provided to the public to help the stakeholders make appropriate decisions about their interest in the organization. The annual reports are used by stakeholders both inside (management) and outside (investors) the organization. Inside the organization, management uses the annual report to evaluate past performance, make new plans, and achieve internal control. Outside the organization, the investors/owners use it to identify and assess investment opportunities and to monitor the condition of their investment.

Generally accepted accounting principles (GAAP) are financial reporting rules that provide consistency and the general framework for the preparation of financial statements. The principles describe the need for the fundamental accounting equation, depreciation, adequate disclosure, and other principles vital for a consistency approach to accounting and financial reports.

Revenue centers are operating departments that produce revenues (sales) by providing products and/or services that generate revenue to clients. Two major examples of revenue centers in the hospitality industry include the food and beverage department and the front office department.

Cost or expense centers are the staff departments that support the operating departments that generate sales. Examples of cost centers include sales and marketing, human resources, engineering and maintenance, security, and accounting departments.

Keywords and Concepts

Accelerated Depreciation	Depreciation
Accounting System	Financial Accounting
Accrual Bases of Accounting	Generally Accepted Accounting Principles (GAAP)
Adequate Disclosure	Internal Control
Annual Report	Managerial Accounting
Audit	Matching Revenues and Expenses
Business Entity Concepts	Money as a Unit of Measure
Cash Bases of Accounting	Night Auditor
Certified Public Accounting (CPA)	Point of Sale (POS)
Consistency Principle	Property Management Systems (PMS)
Cost Accounting	Revenue Centers
Cost or Expense Centers	Straight-line Depreciation
Cost Principle	The Fundamental Accounting Equation

Review Questions

1. What is the difference between financial accounting and managerial accounting?
2. What is the benefit of understanding basic accounting terms and concepts?
3. What is the importance of financial statements?
4. What is the importance of the generally accepted accounting principle (GAAP)?
5. What is depreciation? What is the difference between straight-line depreciation and accelerated depreciation?
6. How do organizations ensure the reliability of the information contained in financial statements?
7. What is the role of an auditor?
8. What is the purpose of internal control?
9. What is the importance of an annual report to an organization's management?
10. Name three stakeholders outside an organization who use an annual report and why they use it?

CHAPTER THREE
Financial Statements

Learning Objectives

After studying this chapter, you should be able to:

1. Discuss the importance of financial statements.
2. Identify hospitality stakeholders and their uses of income statements.
3. Describe an income statement and its uses.
4. Understand the various parts of an income statement.
5. Describe a balance sheet and its uses.
6. Understand the various parts of a balance sheet.
7. Describe a cash flow statement and its uses.
8. Understand the various parts of a cash flow statement.

Importance of Financial Statements

Financial statements inform the management and other stakeholders about the profitability and financial condition of an organization. These statements summarize hundreds, thousands, or even millions of transactions of an organization recorded during the accounting period. It is very essential for managers to understand the general framework for the preparation of financial statements, the contents of these statements, and their uses. The main purpose of financial statements is to provide reliable information to stakeholders and other users for valid evaluation of the financial stability and profitability of a business. Stakeholders need reliable financial statements for deciding where to invest their financial resources. Stakeholders often compare the financial statements of many organizations before deciding where to invest. For the comparisons to be authentic, the financial statements of these diverse organizations should be similar for reasonable comparison. Hence, the financial statements are prepared in a similar format based on generally accepted accounting principles (GAAP).

Stakeholders and Financial Statements

Stakeholders are groups or individuals who have a stake in the form of financial resources, human resources, or other form of assets in an organization or the community where the organization is located. Examples of the hospitality industry's stakeholders and their role in the organization include the following:

- ***Shareholders (Owners):*** Investors who contributed some form of financial resources to own the business.
- ***Managers:*** These are internal stakeholders, individuals inside the organization hired to manage the operations of the organization.
- ***Employees:*** Also internal stakeholders, hired to assist the managers in the daily operations of the organization.
- ***Board of Directors:*** Stakeholders elected to oversee the operations of the business and make executive decisions for the organization.
- ***Creditors:*** Stakeholders who lend money or needed products/services on credit for the operation of the business.
- ***Financial Analysts:*** These are external stakeholders, individuals outside of the organization who analyze financial data for investors or potential investors.
- ***Government Agencies:*** Stakeholders responsible for government regulations and taxation.
- ***Suppliers:*** Stakeholders who provide supplies to business owners for the operation of the business.
- ***Press/Media:*** External stakeholders who provide publicity and keep the public aware of the organization's business practices.
- ***Customers and Community Members:*** Patrons and/or members of the community who patronize the organization or are affected by the presence of the organization in their community.

Many of the stakeholders described above are generally concerned about the impact of the organization on their stake or the community where the organization is located. Some are more interested in the financial statements than others. The stakeholders who are interested in the financial statement use it for various reasons based on their stake in the organization. Exhibit 3.1 lists examples of stakeholders who are users of a hospitality organization's financial statement.

Financial Reporting

Publicly owned corporations are required by law to provide financial data to stakeholders and potential stakeholders. The process of providing financial information to stakeholders outside of the organization is called **financial reporting**. Unlike publicly owned corporations, small businesses are not required by law to provide financial data to stakeholders outside the organization. But they need to maintain accurate and reliable financial statements because stakeholders such as banks and other creditors need these statements as a requirement for granting a loan or other financial assistance. Three sets of financial statements, mostly used in business (including the hospitality industry), are the **income statement** (P&L statement), **balance sheet**, and **cash flow statement**.

Exhibit 3.1: Stakeholders' Uses of Financial Statements

Stakeholders	Uses of Financial Statements
Shareholders (Owners)	To keep track of the progress of their investment and the effectiveness of the managers.
Managers	To keep track of the progress of the organization and use financial data to plan and assess the results of their decisions.
Employees	To help assess the ability of the organization to satisfy wage and benefits requirements.
Board of Directors	To keep track of the organization's progress and the effectiveness of the managers.
Creditors	To ascertain that the organization will be able to pay its debts.
Financial Analysts	To keep track of the organization's progress for its own or clients' investments purposes.
Government Agencies	To monitor the organization's financial performance in regard to taxation and other economic impacts.

"Prosperity is only an instrument to be used, not a deity to be worshipped."
Calvin Coolidge (1872–1933), US president
Source: Speech, Boston, Massachusetts (June 11, 1928)

Income Statement Introduction

The income statement is a financial report that shows the revenue, expenses, and profit or loss of an organization for a specified time period (e.g., a month, quarter, or year). The income statement is also known as a profit and loss (P&L) statement, earning statement, or operating statement. It is used to summarize the profitability of an organization for a specified time period.

In the income statement, net income or net profit is determined by subtracting the cost of goods sold (COGS) and all other operating expenses except taxes from the total sales (revenue). Example 1.3, in Chapter 1, presents a great example of how to determine net income as shown below in Exhibit 3.2. The income statement is a way to show the economic performance of an organization for a specified period. Stakeholders such as business owners, managers, board of directors, financial analysts, and creditors are highly interested in the income statement to see how well the organization is doing.

The net income earned by an organization is a measure of how well the organization is doing. It indicates the economic performance (in terms of profit or loss) of business organizations. The income must be related to a specific **period of time** as indicated in Exhibit 3.2. Notice that the income statement for Charley's Restaurant covers a period of time (for the year ending December 31, 2012). This is vital for a reliable income statement. An income statement cannot be adequately evaluated or analyzed without a specific time period. For example, if a

Exhibit 3.2: Income Statement of Charley's Restaurant

Charley's Restaurant Income Statement For the Year Ended December 31, 2012		
Revenue:	**Dollars**	**Percent**
Food and Beverage	$1,961,875.00	100.00%
Cost of Goods Sold (COGS):		
Food and Beverage	500,000.00	25.49
Gross Profit:	1,461,875.00	74.51
Operating Expenses:		
Payroll and Related Expenses	480,000.00	24.47
Operating Supplies	150,000.00	7.65
Advertising and Promotion	200,000.00	10.19
Repairs and Maintenance	50,000.00	2.55
Energy Costs	120,000.00	6.12
Total Operating Expenses:	1,000,000.00	50.97
Net Income Before Tax	$461,875.00	23.54%

general manager says, "my organization earned a net income of $100,000," the financial or economic performance of the organization is unclear. Did the organization earn $100,000 per month, per quarter, or per year?

The period of time covered by an organization's income statement is termed the organization's **accounting period.** In order to provide all the interested stakeholders and other users of financial statements with timely and comparable information, net income is generally measured in short accounting periods of equal length. This concept is the **time period principle** of the generally accepted accounting principle for the interpretation and preparation of financial statements. The length of an organization's accounting period varies from one organization to another. The accounting period depends upon how frequently the stakeholders and other users need the organization's financial statements. Regardless of the frequency of need, all business organizations are expected to prepare an annual income statement, and most businesses also prepare monthly and quarterly income statements.

Fiscal year is the twelve-month accounting period used by business organizations. The fiscal year used by most business organizations concurs with the calendar year and ends on December 31. Some business organizations, however, may elect to use a fiscal year that ends on a date that is more convenient to the organization.

Parts of an Income Statement

The income statements of the hospitality business are made up of many parts including revenue, cost of goods sold (COGS), gross profit, operating expenses, net profit before tax, and net profit after tax. Later in the subsequent chapter a detailed description of how to prepare an income statement will be presented. The following description of the vital parts of an income statement will be helpful in discussing and preparing an income statement.

Revenue is the price of goods sold and/or the price of the services rendered to consumers during an accounting period. Revenue is interchangeable with **sales**. When a hospitality organization sells its products or renders services to its customers, it's usually paid in the form of cash, checks, or accounts receivable from the customer. The inflow of cash, checks, or accounts receivable increases the total assets of the organization.

Cost of goods sold (COGS) is the cost the hospitality establishment paid for the products or the raw materials used to make the products (e.g., food and beverage) that are sold to its customers. The COGS is actually an expense, but these items are so important that they have to be separated from other expenses in the income statements.

Gross profit is the total sales (revenue) minus the COGS. It is the first tier of profit in an income statement. It is basically the profit generated by the business without the operating costs and taxes.

Net profit before tax is the total sales (revenue) minus the COGS and all other operating expenses except taxes. It is also known as earnings before tax, net income before tax, pretax income, or net operating income before taxes.

Net profit after tax is the total sales (revenue) minus the COGS and all other operating expenses and taxes. It is also known as earnings after tax, net income after tax, or net income.

Uses of Income Statement

- To show the financial performance of business organizations over a specific accounting period (e.g., month or year).
- To record revenues, expenses, and income earned or spent during a specified accounting period.
- By hospitality managers as a guide to monitor the operation of their departments.
- To summarize and measure the profitability of a department and/or an organization for a specified accounting period.

"Civilization and profits go hand in hand."
Calvin Coolidge (1872–1933), US president
Source: Speech (November 1920)

Balance Sheet Introduction

The balance sheet shows the financial status, value, and net worth of an organization at a specific date. It is also referred to as the asset and liability (A&L) statement because it shows the balances of the assets and liabilites, including the difference between the assets and liabilities (owner's equity)—the residual claim of the business entity owner. Most business entities prepare their balance sheets at the end of the month or at the end of their accounting period, and at the end of the year.

The balance sheet must be related to a specific date as indicated in Exhibit 3.3. Notice that the balance sheet for Charley's Restaurant covers a specific date ("For the Year Ended December 31, 2012"). A balance sheet cannot be adequately evaluated or analyzed without a specific date indicating when the organization is valued as reported. Therefore, the date on the balance sheet is very important, as it indicates the financial status, value, and net worth of an organization at that specified date.

Parts of a Balance Sheet

The heading of a balance sheet consists of the name of the business, the name of the financial statement, and the specific date of the balance sheet. The body of the balance sheet is made up of three critical parts: **assets, liabilities,** and **owner's equity.**

Assets

Assets are resources with economic value that are owned by an individual or a business entity, which are expected to provide benefits to future operations. Some examples of assets include cash, inventories, accounts receivable, land, building, etc. The assets can be subdivided into current asset and long-term asset.

Current assets are cash and other assets that can be converted into cash within one year (e.g., cash, accounts receivable, inventories, etc.).

- **Cash** is the money available for use in daily business operations. It can be deposited in a savings or checking account for business operations.
- **Accounts receivable** is the value of the money that is yet to be collected for providing products and/or services to customers. These amounts are expected to be paid generally within a short time. Some examples of accounts receivable include direct billing and credit card purchases.
- **Inventories** are the products or supplies that the organization has purchased but not yet sold or used to provide services to its consumers. Some examples of inventories in a hospitality operation include produce, foodstuffs, beverage, plates, cups, silverwares cleaning supplies, etc. The inventories are assets because the business entity already paid for them, pending when they will be sold and converted into cash.

Exhibit 3.3: Charley's Restaurant Balance Sheet

Charley's Restaurant Balance Sheet For the Year Ended December 31, 2012			
Assets		**Liabilities & Owner's Equity**	
Cash	$ 1,930,000.00	**Liabilities**	
Accounts Receivable	31,875.00	Accounts Payable	$ 520,000.00
Inventories	5,500.00	Payroll and Related Expenses	480,000.00
Supplies	6,300.00	Accrued Expenses	260,500.00
Land	150,000.00	**Total Liabilities**	$ 1,260,500.00
Building	250,000.00	**Owner's Equity**	
Less Depreciation	(120,000.00)	Retained Earning	$ 993,175.00
Total	**$ 2,253,675.00**	**Total**	**$ 2,253,675.00**

Long-term assets are an organization's properties and equipment with more than one year of useful life (e.g., land, building, etc.).

- **Land** is an organization's property that is often purchased for the location of the organization's building. In the hospitality industry, the space occupied by hotels and restaurants is the land.
- **Building** is the physical structure that houses the organization's operations (e.g., the hotel or restaurant building).
- **Equipment** are the machines and other assets used to produce the product or service (e.g., cooking equipment, washers and dryers, computers systems, furniture and fixtures, tables and chairs) used in the organization.
- **Depreciation** is an accounting principle of allocating the cost associated with the purchase of a tangible asset over its estimated useful life.

Liabilities

Liabilities are debts or the amounts owed to creditors for past transactions. Most liability accounts have the word "payable" as part of the account title. Some examples of liabilities include accounts payable, salaries and wages payable, taxes payable, accrued expenses, bank loans, lease obligations, etc. Like assets, liabilities can be subdivided into current liabilities and long-term liabilities.

Current liabilities are debts and other obligations that are less than one year (e.g., accounts payable, tax payable, accrued expenses, etc.).

- **Accounts payable** are the amounts a business entity owes for items or services purchased on credit without a promissory note that need to be paid within a year.
- **Tax payable** is the amount of tax a business entity owes an appropriate tax agency, which is typically paid quarterly or annually.
- **Accrued expenses** are the amounts a business entity owes for business-related purchases or services received but not paid for as agreed.

Long-term liabilities are debts and other obligations of a business entity that are longer than a one-year obligation (e.g., mortgage loan, lease obligation, etc.).

- **Mortgage loans** are real property secured loans through banks or other financial institutions that will be repaid on a regular basis throughout the year, with a duration of usually between five to thirty years.
- **Lease obligations** are a contract to use leased land, a building, or equipment for more than a one-year period.

Owner's equity refers to the owner's claim of the resources with economic value, which are expected to provide benefits to future operations. Owner's equity is the residual amount of what is left after the creditors have been paid. Hence, owner's equity is equal to assets minus liabilities. For example, Exhibit 3.3 shows that the owner's equity is the residual claim of the business entity owner(s), which is secondary to the claims of the creditors (liabilities). It is easier to explain in the equation below:

Formula

3.1. Assets − Liabilities = Owner's Equity
$2,253,675 − $1,260,500 = $993,175

Another way to view this phenomenon: you borrow $1,260,500 to start a business that made $2,253,675 at the end of the business year; your total assets equal $2,253,675, your total liabilities equal $1,260,500, and your equity (owner's equity) equals $993,175 ($2,253,675 − $1,260,500). This is the **fundamental accounting equation**:

Formula

3.2. Assets = Liabilities + Owner's Equity
$2,253,675 = $1,260,500 + $993,175

Uses of Balance Sheet

- To show the financial balances of business organizations at a specific date such as at the end of an accounting period (e.g., end of the month or end of the year).

- To show a business organization's *account activity* and the balance remaining during the specified accounting period.
- By hospitality managers as a guide to monitor the operation of their departments.
- By stakeholders and other users of financial institutions for evaluating the value and net worth of a business entities.

"Drive-in banks were established so most of the cars today could see their real owners."
E. Joseph Cossman (1918–2002), US salesman and entrepreneur
Source: Quoted in The Truth About Money *(Ric Edelman, 2004)*

Cash Flow Statement Introduction

The cash flow statement is the third financial statement used in the assessment of an organization's financial performance. It indicates the liquidity of an organization by providing information about an organization's opening balance, cash receipts, cash disbursement, and closing cash balances during an accounting period.

Opening balance is the amount of cash left in the account of a business entity at the beginning of a new accounting period.

Cash receipts are the amounts of a business entity accounts receivables or sales paid in cash. In the hospitality industry, this includes the amount of food sales, beverage sales, rooms sales, etc. that are paid for in cash or cash equivalent.

Cash disbursements are the amounts of a business entity accounts payables or purchases paid for in cash, such as inventories.

Closing balance is the amount left in the bank account of the business entity after balancing the cash flow statement. Closing balance can be denoted with the following formula:

Formula

3.3.   Closing Balance = Opening Balance + Cash Receipt – Cash Disbursements

---

The **cash flow statement** is one of the financial statements that publicly traded businesses or organizations are required to disclose to stakeholders and other users. It provides information about cash flows. The term **cash flow** refers to cash receipts (inflows) and cash payments or disbursement (outflows). The primary source of cash inflow in a typical hospitality operation is the revenues generated by the organization, which is why the cash flow statement of a typical hospitality organization focuses mainly on the operating activities of the organization. Some of the major characteristics of the cash flow statement are as follows:

- It indicates how liquid an organization is to the stakeholders.
- It starts with a beginning balance and ends with a closing balance.
- It encompasses the cash account of the balance sheet.

- It shows cash receipts (inflows) and cash payments or disbursement (outflows) in the operations of an organization.
- It reflects the increases and decreases in liquidity.
- For major corporations, it has three categories—operating, financing, and investing.

Exhibit 3.4 is a good example of a cash flow statement in the hospitality industry. Notice that the primary source of cash inflow in Charley's Restaurant was food and beverage. You will also notice that the closing balance is based on Formula 3.3, which equals $485,100.25 ($55,100.25 + $ 1,930,000 – $ 1,500,000).

Liquidity

Liquidity can be described as the amount of available cash or cash equivalents that a business entity has to cover its operating expenses. This includes how long it would take the organization to convert the assets of its balance sheet account to cash. A shorter conversion time period reflects a more liquid organization's assets and vice versa. Some examples of liquid assets include the following:

- *Cash* is the most liquid asset of all because it is available for immediate use.
- *Cash equivalents* are the next most liquid asset. These are assets that can be changed to cash in a matter of a few (twenty-four to forty-eight) hours. Examples of cash equivalents include bonds (company and treasury), common stocks, and certificates of deposits (CDs). They are the next most liquid asset because they can be converted to cash (sold) within a short period of time.
- *Liquid assets* are assets in the form of payment in the process of being turned into cash. A good example of liquid asset is accounts receivable, because the payment in cash can be in the organization's account in a matter of a few days.

Importance of Cash Flow Analysis

The importance of cash flow analysis to hospitality managers cannot be overemphasized. A good manager must pay attention to cash inflows as well as cash outflows just as much as she or he pays attention to revenue and profit. Successful mangers find it important to maintain a sufficient amount of cash in their closing bank balance to be able to pay for all necessary operating expenses. For example, if the hospitality manager is not very critical about the amount of cash available in the cash account, then payments—including to vendors, to employees in the form of wages, and to creditors for long-term liabilities (e.g., mortgage loans), all very important for the success of the organization—might become jeopardized. Managers' inability to pay the organization's account payables could also result in bad credit. Creditors and suppliers are not interested in doing business with an organization with bad credit. As a result, the organization may pull the plug and fail.

Exhibit 3.4: Charley's Restaurant Cash Flow Statement

Charley's Restaurant
Cash Flow Statement
For the Year Ended December 31, 2012

	Dollars	Dollars
Opening Balance		$55,100.25
Cash Receipts (Inflows)		
Food and Beverage Sales	$1,479,125.00	
Collection on Account Receivable	450,875.00	
Total Receipts		$ 1,930,000.00
Cash Disbursment (Outflows)		
Food and Beverage Cost	500,000.00	
Payroll and Related Expenses	480,000.00	
Accounts Payable	520,000.00	
Total Disbursement		$ 1,500,000.00
Closing Bank Balance		$485,100.25

"A bank is a place that will lend you money if you can prove that you don't need it."
Bob Hope (1903–2003), US comedian and motion picture actor
Source: *"The Tyranny of Forms,"* Life in the Crystal Palace *(Alan Harrington, 1959)*

Just as it is important to monitor the cash inflow so is it equally important to monitor the cash outflow. Managements are urged to manage the cash account effectively to ensure that no disbursement is made in payment of any debt without enough money in the cash account to cover the debt. Cash increases with more sales in the organization's products/services such as foods, beverages, rooms, etc. But to know whether the sales are cash sales or accounts receivable sales, management must be able to analyze the financial statements with special emphasis on the cash flow statement. For this reason successful managers don't take forms of payment for granted during the closing of daily operations; traveler's checks, individual or company checks, direct bills, and credit card bills are quickly processed as needed until each bill is paid into the cash account.

For the business to survive, it is critical for managers to ensure they are generating positive net cash flow from their establishment's operations. An organization with insufficient cash inflow will not be able to depend on its stakeholders (creditors, banks, etc.) for too long because such stakeholders usually quit investing in those business entities with a negative net cash flow from their operations.

Uses of Cash Flow Statement

Stakeholders use the cash flow statement mostly for assessing the solvency of a business entity. **Solvency** is the ability of a business entity to meet its long-term liabilities and to accomplish long-term expansion. The more solvent a business entity is, the better the business is financially. When a business is insolvent its chances of surviving are futile. Assessing the solvency of a business entity helps stakeholders answer some critical questions, including:

- Is the business solvent? Becoming less solvent or more solvent?
- Is the business operation generating enough cash inflows to pay operating expenses and other liabilities?
- Is the business operation improving in terms of cash flow?

One of management's critical responsibilities is to keep its business establishment solvent. Hence, managers are urged to manage their cash flow by preparing **cash budgets**, which are forecasts of cash inflow and outflow expectations for a specific accounting period. Management can use cash budgets to plan future operation activities and evaluate past operations. The preparation of cash budgets makes management more critical about its operation's cash flows.

Summary

The main purpose of financial statements is to provide reliable information to stakeholders and other users for a valid evaluation of the **financial stability** and **profitability** of a business. Stakeholders need reliable financial statements for deciding where to invest their financial resources. Stakeholders are groups or individuals who have a stake in the form of financial resources, human resources, or other form of assets in an organization or the community where the organization is located.

ACCOUNTING AND FINANCIAL TERMINOLOGY

Accounts payable *are the amounts a business entity owes for items or services purchased on credit without a promissory note that needs to be paid within a year.*

Accounting period *is the period of time covered by an organization's income statement.*

Accounts receivable *is the value of the money that is yet to be collected for providing products and/or services to customers.*

Balance sheet *is a financial report that shows the net worth of an organization in the form of assets, liabilities, and owners' equity at a specific point in time.*

Cash budget *forecasts the cash inflow and outflow expectations for a specific accounting period.*

Cash flow *is a term describing cash receipts (inflows) and cash payments or disbursements (outflows).*

Cash flow statement *is a financial report that shows how much cash is generated, used, and retained by an organization in a specific period.*

Current assets *are cash and other assets that can be converted into cash within one year (e.g., cash, accounts receivable, inventories, etc.).*

Current liabilities *are debts and other obligations that are less than one year (e.g., accounts payable, tax payable, accrued expenses, etc.).*

Financial reporting *is the process of providing financial information to stakeholders outside of the organization.*

Fiscal year *is the twelve-month accounting period used by business organizations. The fiscal year used by most business organizations concurs with the calendar year and ends on December 31.*

Income statement *is a financial report that shows the revenue, expenses, and profit or loss of an organization for a specified time period (e.g., a month, quarter, or year). The income statement is also known as a profit and loss (P&L) statement, earnings statement, or operating statement.*

Liquidity *is the amount of available cash or cash equivalents that a business entity has to cover its operating expenses.*

Long-term assets *are an organization's properties and equipment with more than one year of useful life remaining (e.g., land, building, etc.).*

Long-term liabilities *are debts and other obligations of a business entity that are longer than a one-year obligation (e.g., mortgage loans, lease obligations, etc.).*

Owner's equity *refers to the owner's claim of the resources with economic value, which are expected to provide benefits to future operations.*

Solvency *is the ability of a business entity to meet its long-term liabilities and to accomplish long-term expansion.*

Stakeholders *are groups or individuals who have a stake in the form of financial resources, human resources, or other form of assets in an organization or the community where the organization is located.*

Three sets of financial statements, used mostly in business (including the hospitality industry), are the **income statement** (P&L statement), **balance sheet**, and **cash flow statement**. The income statement of the hospitality business is made up of many parts including revenue, cost of goods sold (COGS), gross profit, operating expenses, net profit before tax, and net profit after tax. The balance sheet is made up of three critical parts: **assets, liabilities,** and **owner's equity.** The **cash flow statement** indicates the liquidity of an organization by providing information about an organization's opening balance, cash receipts, cash disbursements, and closing cash balances during an accounting period.

Keywords and Concepts

Accounting Period	Fiscal Year
Accounts Payable	Gross Profit
Accounts Receivable	Income Statement
Accrued Expenses	Inventories
Balance Sheet	Land
Board of Directors	Lease Obligations
Building Equipment	Liquid Assets
Cash	Liquidity
Cash Budget	Long-Term Assets
Cash Disbursements	Long-Term Liabilities
Cash Equivalents	Long-Term Liabilities
Cash Flow	Managers
Cash Flow Statement	Mortgage Loans
Cash Receipts	Net Profit After Tax
Closing Balance	Net Profit Before Tax
Cost of Goods Sold (COGS)	Opening Balance
Creditors	Owner's Equity
Current Assets	Profitability
Current Liabilities	Revenue
Depreciation	Shareholders (Owners)
Financial Analysts	Solvency
Financial Reporting	Stakeholders
Financial Stability	Tax Payable

Review Questions

1. What is a financial statement? Name five stakeholders in the hospitality industry and their uses of a financial statement.
2. What is a stakeholder? Name five stakeholders in the hospitality industry and their role in the organization.
3. What is the difference between an income statement and a balance sheet?
4. What is the difference between current assets and current liabilities? Give two examples of each.
5. What is the difference between long-term assets and long-term liabilities? Give two examples of each.
6. What is the fundamental account equation?
7. What is the equation for a cash flow statement's closing balance?
8. An investor borrows $2,500,500 to start a business that made $2,990,500 at the end of the fiscal year. Total assets equal $3,200,000, and total liabilities equal $2,500,500. What is the equity (owner's equity) of the investor?

CHAPTER FOUR

Income Statement Preparation

Learning Objectives

After studying this chapter, you should be able to:

1. Understand the importance of a business transaction for income statement preparation.
2. Understand the importance of selecting the right food purveyors.
3. Identify the operating expenses.
4. Understand how to determine profits.
5. Describe and demonstrate the use of the spreadsheet-modeling approach for income statement preparation.

Business Transaction and Income Statement Preparation

The income statement of any business entity is generally limited to the amount of business transactions that occur in the organization. The income statement starts with revenue at the top of the statement (see Exhibit 4.1).

Restaurant **revenue** as shown in Chapter 1 (Formula 1.4) is the multiplication of the average customer expenditure (ACE) by the number of customers served (also described as customer count or volume). Management could find these variables in the business transactions documents (paperwork). All these variables are easily provided by a good point of sale (POS) system.

Similarly, hotel revenue, as shown in Chapter 1 (Formula 1.5), is the multiplication of average daily rate (ADR) by the number of rooms sold (occupancy count). These variables are readily available in a hotel with a property management system (PMS). Once the manager is able to calculate the total revenue or extract it from the POS or PMS system, the next variable in the income statement is the cost of food and beverage sold.

Exhibit 4.1: Income Statement of Charley's Restaurant

<table>
<tr><td colspan="3">Charley's Restaurant
Income Statement
For the Year Ended December 31, 2012</td></tr>
<tr><td>**Revenue:**</td><td>**Dollars**</td><td>**Percent**</td></tr>
<tr><td>Food and Beverage</td><td>$1,961,875.00</td><td>100.00%</td></tr>
<tr><td>**Cost of Goods Sold (COGS):**</td><td></td><td></td></tr>
<tr><td>Food and Beverage</td><td>500,000.00</td><td>25.49</td></tr>
<tr><td>**Gross Profit:**</td><td>1,461,875.00</td><td>74.51</td></tr>
<tr><td>**Operating Expenses:**</td><td></td><td></td></tr>
<tr><td>Payroll and Related Expenses</td><td>480,000.00</td><td>24.47</td></tr>
<tr><td>Operating Supplies</td><td>150,000.00</td><td>7.65</td></tr>
<tr><td>Advertising and Promotion</td><td>200,000.00</td><td>10.19</td></tr>
<tr><td>Repairs and Maintenance</td><td>50,000.00</td><td>2.55</td></tr>
<tr><td>Energy Costs</td><td>120,000.00</td><td>6.12</td></tr>
<tr><td>**Total Operating Expenses:**</td><td>1,000,000.00</td><td>50.97</td></tr>
<tr><td>**Net Income Before Tax**</td><td>$461,875.00</td><td>23.54%</td></tr>
</table>

Selecting the Right Food Purveyors

Food and beverage cost is highly affected by management's choice of food and beverage purveyors. Food and beverage cost in most restaurants is the "cost of goods sold" or "cost of sales." Ordering foodstuffs and beverages from a purveyor with a high cost would raise the food and beverage cost higher than what it would be if ordered from a purveyor with a lesser food and beverage cost. Other things being equal (*ceteris paribus*), the higher the cost of purchasing your foodstuffs and beverage, the higher your food and beverage cost. As such, when selecting food and beverage purveyors, hospitality managers should make the best decision to choose the best value (i.e., the lowest price for the appropriate organization's quality).

When preparing any financial statement in the hospitality industry, management is urged to keep all its numbers in two decimal figures, as shown in Exhibit 4.1. Similarly, the percentages used for comparing the values of the financial statements should also be in two decimal places. Exhibit 4.1 shows that the food and beverage cost percentage is 25.49 percent ($500,000/$1,961,875). This is the division of the food and beverage cost by the sales from food and beverage. In some financial statements, the sales from food will be separated from the sales of beverages. Similarly, the cost of food sold will be separated from the cost of beverages sold. The food cost percentage in such cases is the division of the food cost by the food sales. Similarly, beverage cost percentage is the division of the beverage cost by the beverage sales. It is very important for hospitality managers to understand that food and beverage cost percentages are calculated by using the sales from food and beverage, respectively, and not the total sales or the combination of food and beverage sales. Later in this chapter we shall tackle an example that will clarify this phenomenon.

The gross profit follows the cost of goods sold. Gross profit is the difference between revenue and the cost of goods sold. The next variable after gross profit in the income statement are the operating expenses, as described below.

Operating Expenses

Operating expenses are the costs of the goods and services utilized to earn revenue (sales). Some examples of operating expenses include payroll and related expenses, cost of supplies, advertising and promotion, repairs and maintenance, energy cost, etc. All these costs are necessary for business entities to be able to meet the business goals and objectives of serving customers and earning revenue.

It is very important for managers to be able to differentiate total operating expenses from total expenses. Total operating expense is the addition of all the expenses under operating expenses; whereas, total expense is the addition of the total cost of goods sold plus the total operating expense. The next variable in the income statement are the net profits before and after tax, as described below.

Determining Profit

Net profit before tax as described in Chapter 1 (Formula 1.2) is the total sales (revenue) minus the cost of goods sold (COGS) and all other operating expenses except taxes. It is also known as earnings before tax, net income before tax, pretax income, or net operating income before taxes. Also described in Chapter 1 (Formula 1.3) is the **net profit after tax**, which is the total sales (revenue) minus the cost of goods sold (COGS) and all other operating expenses and taxes. It is also known as earnings after tax, net income after tax, or net income.

To calculate net profit after tax, you have to be aware of the tax rate per income bracket. For example, the United States uses the progressive tax system. Progressive tax basically means the more income you make within a certain income bracket, the more tax you pay.

Tax rate could vary from year to year depending on government policies and regulations. Hence, managers are highly encouraged to be aware of the appropriate tax rate applicable to their income bracket when preparing the income statement. Now that you are familiar with preparation of the income statement, the following example will illustrate the preparation of an income statement using a spreadsheet-modeling approach.

Spreadsheet-Modeling Approach for Income Statement Preparation

EXAMPLE 4.1

Scenario: As Paradise Restaurant manager, you are asked to present a P&L (income) statement of the previous month to your stakeholders at the board meeting. You have only forty-eight hours to ensure that the information in the P&L statement is accurate. Fortunately for your organization, you are good at keeping the operation's records. Twenty-four hours prior to your presentation you collected the following information:

Question: Use the spreadsheet-modeling approach to prepare an income statement for December using the information in Exhibit 4.2.

ANSWER: To solve this question, you need to be familiar with some formulas as outlined below (Formulas 4.1–4.10). Remember the spreadsheet design guiding principles in Chapter 1, as listed in Exhibit 4.3, then follow the step-by-step, hands-on approach to Example 4.1 as outlined below.

Exhibit 4.2: Paradise Business Transaction for December

Variables	Dollars
Food Sales	$ 80,514.00
Beverage Sales	$ 4,968.00
Food Cost	$ 27,374.76
Beverage Cost	$ 1,341.36
Operating Expenses	
Payroll and Related Expenses	$ 26,499.42
Employee Meals	$ 1,282.23
Operating Supplies	$ 8,548.20
Administration and General	$ 1,282.23
Advertising and Promotion	$ 1,709.64
Repairs and Maintenance	$ 1,709.64
Energy Cost	$ 3,419.28

Formulas

4.1. Total Sales = Food Sales + Beverage Sales.

4.2. Total Cost of Sales = Food Cost + Beverage Cost

4.3. Gross Profit = Total Sales − Total Cost of Sales

4.4. Total Operating Expenses = The Sum of All the Operating Expenses

4.5. Income Before Tax = Gross Profit − Total Operating Expenses

4.6. Food Cost Percentage $= \dfrac{\text{Food Cost}}{\text{Food Sales}}$

4.7. Beverage Cost Percentage $= \dfrac{\text{Beverage Cost}}{\text{Beverage Sales}}$

4.8. Total Cost of Sales Percentage $= \dfrac{\text{Total Cost of Sales}}{\text{Total Sales (Revenue)}}$

4.9. Food Sales Percentage $= \dfrac{\text{Food Sales}}{\text{Total Sales (Revenue)}}$

4.10. Expense Percentage $= \dfrac{\text{Expense}}{\text{Total Sales (Revenue)}}$

Exhibit 4.3: Spreadsheet Design Guiding Principles

1. **Organize the data using the given variables**: It is critical to arrange the variables in a visually pleasing manner (i.e., series of the each variable in one column or row) for an easy understanding and location of the variables. A good organization of the variable will also enhance the credibility and auditability of the spreadsheet model.

2. **Incorporate cells in your formulas:** A design that incorporates cells in formulas that can be copied to do a series of calculations is more understandable and less prone to mistakes than the alternatives. Once the first formula is done correctly, it can be copied to solve the other series of calculations. In addition, if there is a mistake in data entering, once the mistake is corrected the calculations would be automatically corrected.

3. **Keep total at the end of a column or row:** It is very common for spreadsheet users to expect the number at the end of a column or row to be the total of the calculation of the data in that column or row. Numbers that do not represent the total of a column or row should be clearly labeled to prevent misinterpretation of the column or row.

4. **Data entry design:** It is common for data entry in the spreadsheet to be from top to bottom and left to right. This should be considered when designing a spreadsheet to enhance the consistency, readability, and auditability of the spreadsheet model.

5. Distinguish changeable columns or rows: Use shading, borders, and/or colors to distinguish changeable columns or rows of variables. This makes it easy to identify and modify the columns or rows in case of a mistake.

6. **Create text boxes with cell notes**: Use text boxes and cell notes to keep a record of how each decision variable in the spreadsheet model was calculated. This will enhance the understanding and auditability of the spreadsheet model.

7. **The use of equal sign (=)**: When starting a calculation in Excel spreadsheet, the first thing to type into the "cell" that tells Excel to calculate is the equal sign (=).

Now that you are familiar with critical formulas needed to solve the example 4.1 and you have refreshed your memory about the spreadsheet design guiding principles, follow the step-by-step, hands-on approach to Example 4.1 as outlined below:

STEP-BY-STEP, HANDS-ON APPROACH TO EXAMPLE 4.1

1. In your Excel spreadsheet, label cells B1, C1, and D1 as *Variable*, *Dollars*, and *Percentage*, respectively, as the headings.

2. Insert the given variables (food sales, beverage sales, food cost, etc. under variables) and insert the appropriate dollar value for each variable in the appropriate cell under the *Dollars* heading.

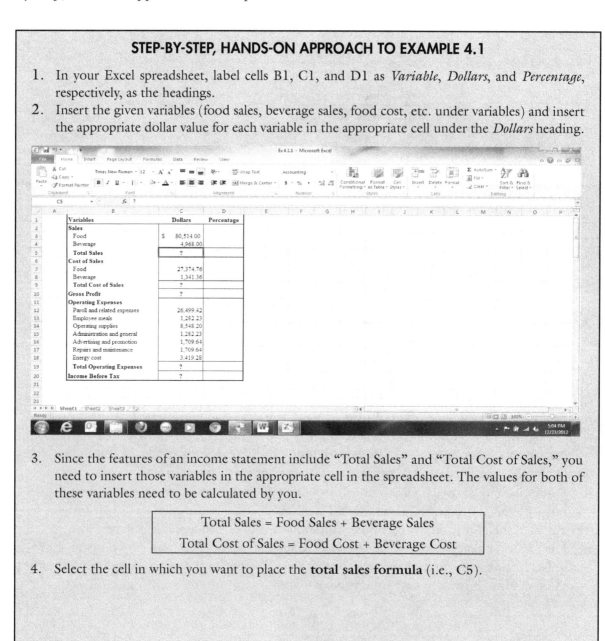

3. Since the features of an income statement include "Total Sales" and "Total Cost of Sales," you need to insert those variables in the appropriate cell in the spreadsheet. The values for both of these variables need to be calculated by you.

> Total Sales = Food Sales + Beverage Sales
>
> Total Cost of Sales = Food Cost + Beverage Cost

4. Select the cell in which you want to place the **total sales formula** (i.e., C5).

5. Type an equal sign (=) to start the formula. Click the first cell you want to place in the formula (i.e., C3). When you click the cell, a border surrounds the cell indicating the cell you are working with and its name appears on the formula bar. Next, type the plus (+) key to the formula bar to form [=C3+]. Click the second cell you want to place in the formula (i.e., C4) to form [=C3+C4], then press the enter key. Excel calculates the result and displays it in the cell as **$85,482**.

6. Select the cell in which you want to place the **food cost formula** (i.e., C9).

7. Type an equal sign (=) to start the formula. Click the first cell you want to place in the formula (i.e., C7). When you click the cell, a border surrounds the cell indicating the cell you are working with and its name appears on the formula bar. Next, type the plus (+) key to the formula bar to form [=C7+]. Click the second cell you want to place in the formula (i.e., C8) to form [=C7+C8], then press the enter key. Excel calculates the result and displays it in the cell as **$28,716.12**.

8. The next variable you need to insert in the appropriate spreadsheet cell is *Gross Profit*.

> Gross profit = Total Sales – Total Cost of Sales

9. Select the cell in which you want to place the **gross profit formula** (i.e., C10).

10. Type an equal sign (=) to start the formula. Click the first cell you want to place in the formula (i.e., C5). When you click the cell, a border surrounds the cell indicating the cell you are working with and its name appears on the formula bar. Next, type the minus (–) key to the formula bar to form [=C5–]. Click the second cell you want to place in the formula (i.e., C9) to form [=C5 – C9], then press the enter key. Excel calculates the result and displays it in the cell as **$56,756.88**.

11. The next variable you need to insert in the appropriate spreadsheet cell is *Total Operating Expenses*.

> Total Operating Expenses = The Sum of All the Operating Expenses

12. Select the cell in which you want to place the **total operating expenses formula** (i.e., C19).

13. Type an equal sign (=) to start the formula. Since you are adding more than two variables, you could use the sum function to make it faster. Hence, type in SUM after the equal sign (=) followed with an open parenthesis to form [=SUM( ]. Select the cells you want to sum up in the formula (i.e., C12:C18). When you select the cells, a border surrounds the cells indicating the cell you are summing up, which will appear on the formula bar. Next, insert the close parenthesis to form [=SUM(C12:C18)], then press the enter key. Excel calculates the result and displays it in the cell as **$44,450.64**.

14. The next variable you need to insert in the appropriate spreadsheet cell is *Income Before Tax*.

> Income Before Tax = Gross Profit - Total Operating Expenses

15. Select the cell in which you want to place the **income before tax formula** (i.e., C20).

16. Type an equal sign (=) to start the formula. Click the first cell you want to place in the formula (i.e., C10). When you click the cell, a border surrounds the cell indicating the cell you are working with and its name appears on the formula bar. Next, type the minus (–) key to the formula bar to form [=C10–]. Click the second cell you want to place in the formula (i.e., C19) to form [=C10 – C19], then press the enter key. Excel calculates the result and displays it in the cell as **$12,315.24**.

17. Now that you are done calculating all the necessary variables in the *Dollars* column, it is time to calculate the percentages for each variable.
18. Let us start with the *Food Sales Percentage*.

$$\text{Food Sales Percentage} = \frac{\text{Food Sales}}{\text{Total Sales (Revenue)}}$$

19. Select the cell in which you want to place the **food sales percentage formula** (i.e., D3).
20. Type an equal sign (=) to start the formula. Click the first cell you want to place in the formula (i.e., C3). When you click the cell, a border surrounds the cell indicating the cell you are working with and its name appears on the formula bar. Next, type the slash (/) key to the formula bar to form [=C3/]. Click the second cell you want to place in the formula (i.e., C5) to form [=C3/C5]. To make this formula applicable to more cells, insert the dollar sign ($) in front of the C and 5 of C5 to form [=C3/$C$5], then press the enter key. Excel calculates the result and displays it in the cell as **0.94188**.
21. Since this is supposed to be in percentage, click the percentage (%) sign in the Excel tool bar. Excel calculates the result and displays it in the cell. If you limit your result to two decimal places you will have **94.19%**.
22. To calculate the rest of the percentages, just copy the cell D3 (94.19%) and paste it into any of the cells you want to calculate except when calculating for food cost and beverage cost percentages.
23. To calculate the *Food Cost Percentage* use the formula below (4.6).

$$\text{Food Cost Percentage} = \frac{\text{Food Cost}}{\text{Food Sales}}$$

24. Select the cell in which you want to place the **food cost percentage formula** (i.e., D7).
25. Type an equal sign (=) to start the formula. Click the first cell you want to place in the formula (i.e., C7). When you click the cell, a border surrounds the cell indicating the cell you are working with and its name appears on the formula bar. Next, type the slash (/) key to the formula bar to form [=C7/]. Click the second cell you want to place in the formula (i.e., C3) to form [=C7/C3], then press the enter key. Excel calculates the result and displays **0.3400** in the cell.
26. Click the percentage (%) sign in the Excel tool bar. Excel calculates the result and displays it in the cell. If you limit your result to two decimal places you will have **34.00%**.
27. To calculate the *Beverage Cost Percentage* use the formula below (4.7).

$$\text{Beverage Cost Percentage} = \frac{\text{Beverage Cost}}{\text{Beverage Sales}}$$

28. Select the cell in which you want to place the **beverage cost percentage formula** (i.e., D8).
29. Type an equal sign (=) to start the formula. Click the first cell you want to place in the formula (i.e., C8). When you click the cell, a border surrounds the cell indicating the cell you are working with and its name appears on the formula bar. Next, type the slash (/) key to the formula bar to form [=C8/]. Click the second cell you want to place in the formula (i.e., C4) to form [=C8/C4], then press the enter key. Excel calculates the result and displays it in the cell as **0.2700**.

30. Click the percentage (%) sign in the Excel tool bar. Excel calculates the result and displays it in the cell. If you limit your result to two decimal places you will have **27.00%**.
31. Again, to calculate the rest of the percentages, just copy the cell D3 (94.19%) and paste it into any of the cells you want to calculate except when calculating for food cost and beverage cost percentages.
32. By following these instructions you should be done preparing an income statement for the board in a short time.
33. If you make any mistakes in typing any of numbers, do not panic. This is one of the advantages of the spreadsheet-modeling approach to financial analysis. Just make the necessary changes and all the calculations will be automatically corrected.

The answer to Example 4.1 in the spreadsheet-modeling approach is displayed in Exhibit 4.4. If your spreadsheet answers are different from the answers as shown in Exhibit 4.4, do not despair. Just locate your mistake and correct the specific cell(s). Exhibit 4.4 of the spreadsheet model of Example 4.1 did not include the identity and the accounting period of the income statement. These are important components of an income statement. Exhibit 4.4 mainly focused on solving the questions. Exhibit 4.5, however, shows the identity and the accounting period of the income statement, just as it should be included in all income statements before or after the preparation of these statements.

Exhibit 4.4: Spreadsheet-Modeling Approach to Example 4.1

Variables	Dollars	Percentage
Sales		
Food	$ 80,514.00	94.19%
Beverage	4,968.00	5.81%
Total Sales	**$ 85,482.00**	**100.00%**
Cost of Sales		
Food	27,374.76	34.00%
Beverage	1,341.36	27.00%
Total Cost of Sales	28,716.12	33.59%
Gross Profit	**$ 56,765.88**	**66.41%**
Operating Expenses		
Paroll and related expenses	26,499.42	31.00%
Employee meals	1,282.23	1.50%
Operating supplies	8,548.20	10.00%
Administration and general	1,282.23	1.50%
Advertising and promotion	1,709.64	2.00%
Repairs and maintenance	1,709.64	2.00%
Energy cost	3,419.28	4.00%
Total Operating Expenses	**44,450.64**	**52.00%**
Income Before Tax	**$ 12,315.24**	**14.41%**

Exhibit 4.5: Spreadsheet-Modeling Approach to Example 4.1 with Identity

Paradise Restaurant		
Income Statement		
For the Month Ended December 31, 2012		
Variables	**Dollars**	**Percentage**
Sales		
Food	$ 80,514.00	94.19%
Beverage	4,968.00	5.81%
Total Sales	$ 85,482.00	100.00%
Cost of Sales		
Food	27,374.76	34.00%
Beverage	1,341.36	27.00%
Total Cost of Sales	28,716.12	33.59%
Gross Profit	$ 56,765.88	66.41%
Operating Expenses		
Paroll and related expenses	26,499.42	31.00%
Employee meals	1,282.23	1.50%
Operating supplies	8,548.20	10.00%
Administration and general	1,282.23	1.50%
Advertising and promotion	1,709.64	2.00%
Repairs and maintenance	1,709.64	2.00%
Energy cost	3,419.28	4.00%
Total Operating Expenses	44,450.64	52.00%
Income Before Tax	$ 12,315.24	-14.41%

ACCOUNTING AND FINANCIAL TERMINOLOGY

Ceteris paribus *is a term used to refer to "other things equal," basically used to describe a relationship when other conditions of that relationship remain the same.*

Cost of sales *is the cost the hospitality establishment paid for the products or the raw materials used to make the products (e.g., food and beverage) that are sold to its customers.*

Income statement *is a financial report that shows the revenue, expenses, and profit or loss of an organization for a specified time period (e.g., a month, quarter, or year). The income statement is also known as a profit and loss (P&L) statement, earnings statement, or operating statement.*

Gross profit *is the difference between revenue and the cost of goods sold.*

Net profit after tax *is the total sales (revenue) minus the cost of goods sold (COGS) and all other operating expenses and taxes.*

Net profit before tax *is the total sales (revenue) minus the cost of goods sold (COGS) and all other operating expenses except taxes.*

Operating expenses *are the costs of the goods and services utilized to earn revenue (sales).*

Summary

The preparation of the income statement starts with *revenue* at the top of the statement. The revenue or total sales is followed by the *cost of food and beverage sold* (cost of sales). *Gross profit* follows the cost of sales. Gross profit is the difference between revenue and the cost of sales. The next variable after gross profit in the income statement is *operating expenses* followed by *income before tax* (net profit before tax).

Keywords and Concepts

Accounting Period

Ceteris Paribus

Cost of Sales

Gross Profit

Income Statement

Net Profit After Tax

Net Profit Before Tax

Operating Expenses

Profitability

Revenue

Tax Rate

Review Questions

1. The following data are adapted from a monthly income statement of Charley's Restaurant. Compute the percentages for each variable?

Variables	Dollars	Percentage
Total Sales	$120,600.00	
Total Cost of Sales	35,950.00	
Gross Profit	84,650.00	
Total Operating Expenses	59,893.00	
Income Before Tax	24,757.00	

I. What is Charley's Restaurant's total revenue percentage?
II. What is Charley's Restaurant's total cost of sales percentage?
III. What is Charley's Restaurant's gross profit percentage?
IV. What is Charley's Restaurant's total operating expense percentage?
V. What is Charley's Restaurant's income before tax percentage?

2. **Scenario**: As a restaurant manager at Charley's Restaurant, you are asked to present a P&L (income) statement of the previous month to your stakeholders at the board meeting, using the following information:

Charley's Restaurant's Business Transaction for January

Variables	Dollars
Food Sales	$ 105,000.00
Beverage Sales	$ 5600.00
Food Cost	$ 34,200.00
Beverage Cost	$ 1,550.00
Operating Expenses	
Payroll and Related Expenses	$ 28,501.00
Employee Meals	$ 1,420.00
Operating Supplies	$ 10,520.00
Administration and General	$ 1,450.00
Advertising and Promotion	$ 2,100.00
Repairs and Maintenance	$ 3,200.00
Energy Cost	$ 5,102.00

Question: Use the spreadsheet-modeling approach to prepare a financial statement for December using the above information and answer the following questions.

I.   What is Charley's Restaurant's total revenue percentage?
II. What is Charley's Restaurant's total cost of sales?
III. What is Charley's Restaurant's gross profit?
IV. What is Charley's Restaurant's total operating expense?
V.   What is Charley's Restaurant's income before tax?

CHAPTER FIVE

Balance Sheet and Cash Flow Statement Preparation

Learning Objectives

After studying this chapter, you should be able to:

1. Describe a balance sheet.
2. Identify assets and liabilities.
3. Calculate the owner's equity.
4. Demonstrate the use of the spreadsheet-modeling approach for balance sheet preparation.
5. Describe a cash flow statement.
6. Identify the variables of a cash flow statement termed Receipts.
7. Identify the variables of a cash flow statement termed Disbursements.
8. Demonstrate the use of the spreadsheet-modeling approach for cash flow statement preparation.

A **balance sheet** is also known as an **asset and liability (A&L)** statement. It shows the financial status, value, and net worth of an organization at a specific date. The body of the balance sheet is made up of assets, liabilities, and owner's equity. The income (P&L) statement provides information that is connected to the balance sheet (A&L statement). Hospitality managers who understand the relationships between the balance sheet and the P&L statement will be able to use these financial statements to effectively enhance their organization's operation.

Identifying Assets and Liabilities

Assets (as described in Chapter 3) are resources with economic value that are owned by an individual or a business entity, and which are expected to provide benefits to future operations. Some examples of assets include cash, inventories, accounts receivable, land, building, etc. The best way to identify an asset is to examine the given variable and ask the following questions:

- Is the variable cash or cash receivable?
- Can the variable be converted into cash in the short or long run?
- Can the variable be used to generate cash in the short or long run?

If the answer to any of the above questions is "yes," then the variable is an asset. All the variables identified to be assets should be placed under the assets column of the balance sheet and added up to determine the total value of assets.

Liabilities (as described in Chapter 3) are debts or the amounts owed to creditors for past transactions. Most liability accounts have the word "payable" as part of the account title. Some examples of liabilities include accounts payable, salaries and wages payable, taxes payable, accrued expenses, bank loans, lease obligations, etc. Like assets, the best way to identify a liability is to examine the given variable and ask the following questions:

- Is the variable going to cost or take money away from the business?
- Does the variable require money from the business in the short or long run?
- Is the variable part of the expenses needed for the business?

If the answer to any of the above questions is "yes," then the variable is a liability. All the variables identified to be liabilities should be placed under the liabilities column of the balance sheet and added up to determine the total value of liabilities. If the assets and liabilities are identified, arranged in their respective column and calculated appropriately, calculating the owner's equity won't be a difficult task.

Calculating the Owner's Equity

Owner's equity is basically equal to assets minus liabilities, a derivative of the fundamental accounting equation. It is easier to explain in the equation below:

$$\text{Assets} - \text{Liabilities} = \text{Owner's Equity}$$
$$\$2,000,000 - \$1,500,000 = \$500,000$$

Another way to view this phenomenon: You borrow $1.5 million to start a business that made $2 million at the end of the business year. Your total assets equal $2 million, your total liabilities equal $1.5 million, and your equity (owner's equity) equals $500,000 ($2,000,000 − $1,500,000). This is the **fundamental accounting equation**:

$$\text{Assets} = \text{Liabilities} + \text{Owner's equity}$$
$$\$2,000,000 = \$1,500,000 + \$500,000$$

Now that you can identify assets, liabilities, and calculate the owner's equity, the following example will illustrate the preparation of a balance sheet using a spreadsheet-modeling approach.

Spreadsheet-Modeling Approach for Balance Sheet Preparation

EXAMPLE 5.1

Scenario: Charles is the owner and general manager of Charley's Restaurant. He gathered and gave the information in Exhibit 5.1 to his restaurant manager to prepare the balance sheet for the establishment as of January 31.

Question: If you are the restaurant manager of Charley's Restaurant, solve the following:
I.   Arrange the given information into assets and liabilities.
II. Use a spreadsheet-modeling approach (using the information in Exhibit 5.1) to prepare a balance sheet for January, computing the total assets, total current liabilities, total liabilities, owner's equity, and total liabilities and owner's equity of the business to date.

ANSWER: To solve this question, you need to be familiar with basic arithmetic and equations as shown below, remember the spreadsheet design guiding principles in Chapter 1 (as listed in Exhibit 4.3), and then follow the step-by-step, hands-on approach to Example 5.1 as outlined below.

Exhibit 5.1

Variables	Dollars
Cash in bank	$ 12,135.96
Accounts receivable	28,258.80
Inventories	16,373.88
Accounts payable	28,141.56
Prepaid rent	652.56
Accrued property tax	12610.80
Prepaid advertising	898.80
Prepaid insurance	2,329.56
Advance payment	8,891.52
Accrued utilities	6,373.44
Furniture and equipment	47,907.36
Operating equipment	6,555.84
Accumulated depreciation	-1,764.84
Accrued payroll	23239.80
Long-term debt	21,002.76
Accrued credit card commission	3,093.12

Formulas

5.1.   Assets = Liabilities + Owner's Equity.
5.2.   Assets – Liabilities = Owner's Equity.
5.3.   Total Assets = The Sum of All the Assets
5.4.   Total Liabilities = The Sum of All the Liabilities

STEP-BY-STEP, HANDS-ON APPROACH TO EXAMPLE 5.1

1. In your Excel spreadsheet, start with the identity of the balance sheet by inserting *Charley's Restaurant*, *Balance Sheet*, and *January 31, 2012* in rows 1, 2, and 3, respectively, as follows:

> Charley's Restaurant
> Balance Sheet
> January 31, 2012

2. In your Excel spreadsheet, label cells B4, C4, E4, and F4 as *Assets*, *Dollars*, *Liabilities and Owner's Equity*, and *Dollars*, respectively, as the headings.
3. Separate the given variables into assets and liabilities and insert the appropriate dollar value for each variable in the appropriate cell under the *Dollars* headings.

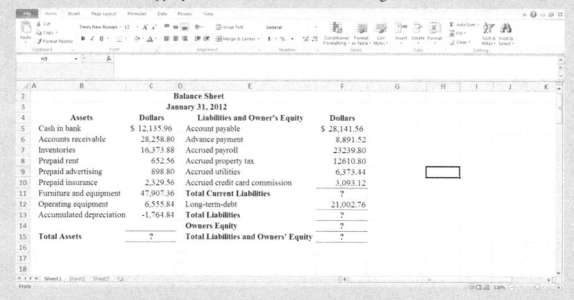

4. Select the cell in which you want to place the **total assets formula** (i.e., C15).
5. Type an equal sign (=) to start the formula. Since you are adding more than two variables, you could use the sum function to make it faster. Hence, type in SUM after the equal sign (=) followed with an open parenthesis to form [=SUM ( ]. Select the cells you want to sum up in the formula (i.e., C5:C13). When you select the cells, a border surrounds the cells indicating the cell you are summing up, which will appear on the formula bar. Next, insert the close parenthesis to form [=SUM (C5:C13)], then press the enter key. Excel calculates the result and displays it in the cell as **$113,347.92**.

6. The next variable you need to insert in the appropriate spreadsheet cell is *Total Current Liabilities*.

7. Similarly, select the cell in which you want to place the **total current liabilities formula** (i.e., F11).

8. Type an equal sign (=) to start the formula. Since you are adding more than two variables, you could use the sum function to make it faster. Hence, type in SUM after the equal sign (=) followed with an open parenthesis to form [=SUM ( ]. Select the cells you want to sum up in the formula (i.e., F5:F10). When you select the cells, a border surrounds the cells indicating the cell you are summing up, which will appear on the formula bar. Next, insert the close parenthesis to form [=SUM (F5:F10)], then press the enter key. Excel calculates the result and displays it in the cell as **$82,350.24**.

9. The next variable you need to insert in the appropriate cell in the spreadsheet is *Total Liabilities*.

10. Similarly, select the cell in which you want to place the **total liabilities formula**(i.e., F13).

11. Type an equal sign (=) to start the formula. Click the first cell you want to place in the formula (i.e., F11). When you click the cell, a border surrounds the cell indicating the cell you are working with and its name appears on the formula bar. Next, type the plus (+) key to the formula bar to form [=F11+]. Click the second cell you want to place in the formula (i.e., F12) to form [=F11+F12], then press the enter key. Excel calculates the result and displays it in the cell as **$103,353**.

12. The next variable you need to insert in the appropriate spreadsheet cell is *Owner's Equity*.

Assets – Liabilities = Owner's Equity

13. Select the cell in which you want to place the **owner's equity formula** (i.e., F14)

14. Type an equal sign (=) to start the formula. Click the first cell you want to place in the formula (i.e., C15). When you click the cell, a border surrounds the cell indicating the cell you are working with and its name appears on the formula bar. Next, type the minus (–) key to the formula bar to form [=C15–]. Click the second cell you want to place in the formula (i.e., F13) to form [=C15 – F13], then press the enter key. Excel calculates the result and displays it in the cell as **$9,994.92**.

15. The next variable you need to insert in the appropriate spreadsheet cell is *Liabilities and Owner's Equity*.

Assets = Liabilities + Owner's Equity

16. Select the cell in which you want to place the **liabilities and owner's equity formula** (i.e., F15).

17. Type an equal sign (=) to start the formula. Click the first cell you want to place in the formula (i.e., F13). When you click the cell, a border surrounds the cell indicating the cell you are working with and its name appears on the formula bar. Next, type the plus (+) key to the formula bar to form [=F13+]. Click the second cell you want to place in the formula (i.e., F14) to form [=F13+F14], then press the enter key. Excel calculates the result and displays it in the cell as **$113,347.92**.

18. By following these instructions you should be done preparing the balance sheet for the month of January, computing the total assets, total current liabilities, total liabilities, owner's equity, and total liabilities and owner's equity of the business to date.

19. Again, if you make any mistakes in typing any of the numbers do not panic. Just make the necessary changes and all the calculations will be automatically corrected.

The answer to Example 5.1 using the spreadsheet-modeling approach is displayed in Exhibit 5.2. If your spreadsheet answers are different from the answers as shown in Exhibit 5.2, do not despair. Just locate your mistake and correct the specific cell(s).

Exhibit 5.2: Spreadsheet-Modeling Approach to Example 5.1

	Charley's Restaurant					
	Balance Sheet					
	January 31, 2012					
Assets			Liabilities and Owner's Equity			
Cash in bank	$ 12,135.96		Account payable		$ 28,141.56	
Accounts receivable	28,258.80		Advance payment		8,891.52	
Inventories	16,373.88		Accrued payroll		23239.80	
Prepaid rent	652.56		Accrued property tax		12610.80	
Prepaid advertising	898.80		Accrued utilities		6,373.44	
Prepaid insurance	2,329.56		Accrued credit card commission		3,093.12	
Furniture and equipment	47,907.36		Total Current Liabilities		$ 82,350.24	
Operating equipment	6,555.84		Long-term-debt		21,002.76	
Accumulated depreciation	-1,764.84		Total Liabilities		$ 103,353.00	
			Owners Equity		$ 9,994.92	
Total Assets	$ 113,347.92		Total Liabilities and Owners' Equity		$ 113,347.92	

Cash Flow Statement

Cash flow statement refers to cash receipts (inflows) and cash payments or disbursements (outflows). The primary source of cash inflow in a typical hospitality operation is the revenues generated by the organization. Cash flow statements usually start with the opening balance, which is the amount of cash money left in the account of a business entity at the beginning of a new accounting period, and ends with the closing balance, which is the amount left in the bank account of the business entity after balancing the cash flow statement. The income (P&L) statement provides information that is connected to the cash flow statement. Hospitality managers who understand the relationships between the P&L and cash flow statement will be able to use these financial statements to effectively enhance the liquidity of her or his organization.

Identifying Cash Flow Receipts

Cash flow "receipts" are cash inflows to the business. As described in Chapter 3, receipts are the amounts of a business entity's accounts receivables or sales paid in cash. This includes cash or cash equivalents that a business entity receives in return for its products/services. The best way to identify receipts is to examine each given variable and ask the following questions:

- Is the variable cash?
- Is the variable debit or credit sales collected?
- Is the variable cash receivable collected?

If the answer to any of the above questions is "yes," then the variable is a receipt. All the variables identified to be receipts should be placed under the receipts column of the cash flow statement and added up to determine the total value of the receipts.

Identifying Cash Flow Disbursements

Cash flow "disbursements" are cash payments or outflows. As described in Chapter 3, disbursements are the amounts of a business entity's accounts payable or purchases paid for in cash, such as inventories. The best way to identify disbursements is to examine each given variable and ask the following questions:

- Is the variable cost of sales payable in cash?
- Is the variable operating expense payable in cash?
- Is the variable account payable due?

If the answer to any of the above questions is "yes," then the variable is a disbursement. All the variables identified to be disbursements should be placed under the disbursements column of the cash flow statement and added up to determine the total value of the disbursements.

Now that you are familiar with the cash flow statement, the following example will illustrate the preparation of a cash flow statement using a spreadsheet-modeling approach.

Spreadsheet-Modeling Approach for Cash Flow Statement Preparation

EXAMPLE 5.2

Scenario: Charles is the owner and general manager of Charley's Restaurant. He gathered and gave the income and expense information in Exhibit 5.3 to his restaurant manager to prepare the cash flow statement for the establishment as of January 31.

Question: As the restaurant manager of Charley's Restaurant, in addition to the above information you are informed that the cash sales percentages are 85 for food and 85 for beverage. Sixty percent of the $15,350 credit sales in Charley's Restaurant's December accounts receivable were collected. Twenty percent of the January cost of food and 90 percent of the cost of beverage were paid in cash, 100 percent of all the operating expenses were paid in cash, and 80 percent of accounts payable for December's $25,500 F&B purchases were paid in January. Solve the following:

    I.   Arrange the given information into receipts and disbursements.

II. Use the spreadsheet-modeling approach (using the information in Exhibit 5.3) to prepare a cash flow statement for January, computing the total receipts, total disbursements, and net cash flow (closing bank balance) of the business to date. The opening cash balance on January 1 was $135,255.

ANSWER: To solve this question, you need to be familiar with basic arithmetic formulas, remember the spreadsheet design guiding principles in Chapter 1 (as listed in Exhibit 4.3), be able to identify the receipts and disbursements, and then follow the step-by-step, hands-on approach to Example 5.2 as outlined below.

Exhibit 5.3

Variable	Dollars
Food revenue	$80,514.00
Beverage revenue	4,968.00
Food cost	27,374.76
Beverage cost	1,341.36
Payroll and related expenses	26,499.42
Employee meals	1,282.23
Operating supplies	8,548.20
Administration and general	1,282.23
Advertising and promotion	1,709.64
Repairs and maintenance	1,709.64
Energy cost	3,419.28

Formulas

5.5. Cash Inflow = Dollars × Cash Inflow Percentage

5.6. Cash Outflow = Dollars × Cash Outflow Percentage

5.7. Net Cash Flow = Opening Balance + Total Receipt – Total Disbursement

5.8. Total Receipts = The Sum of All the Cash Inflows

5.9. Total Disbursement = The Sum of All the Cash Outflows

STEP-BY-STEP, HANDS-ON APPROACH TO EXAMPLE 5.2

1. In your Excel spreadsheet, start with the identity of the balance sheet by inserting *Charley's Restaurant*, *Cash Flow Statement*, and *For the Month Ended January 31, 2012* in rows 1, 2, and 3, respectively, as follows:

> Charley's Restaurant
> Cash Flow Statement
> For the Month Ended January 31, 2012

2. In your Excel spreadsheet, label cells C4, D4, and E4 as *Dollars, Cash Flow %*, and *Cash Flow*, respectively, as the headings.
3. Label cells B5 and B6 *Opening Balance* and *Receipts*, respectively, as subheadings.
4. Identify all the receipts, list each of them per cell below the receipts subheading, and insert the appropriate dollar value for each variable in the appropriate cell under the *Dollars* headings. Similarly, insert the appropriate cash flow percentage in the appropriate cell under *Cash Flow %*.
5. Then, compute the cash inflow by multiplying the dollar value of each receipt by its cash inflow percentage.

> Cash Inflow = Dollars × Cash Inflow Percentage

6. Select the cell in which you want to place the **cash from food sales formula** (i.e., E7).
7. Type an equal sign (=) to start the formula. Click the first cell you want to place in the formula (i.e., C7). When you click the cell, a border surrounds the cell indicating the cell you are working with and its name appears on the formula bar. Next, type the asterisk (*) key to the formula bar to form [=C7*]. Click the second cell you want to place in the formula (i.e., D7) to form [=C7*D7], then press the enter key. Excel calculates the result and displays it in the cell as **$68,436.90**.
8. At this point of the calculation, you could copy cell E7 and paste it to E8 and E9 to compute similar calculations for "Cash from beverage sales" and "Cash from account receivable," respectively (or repeat steps 7 and 8 for each). If you copy and paste correctly, "Cash from beverage sales" and "Cash from account receivable" will be **$4,222.80 (E8)** and **$9,210 (E9)**, respectively (copying and pasting like this is one of the advantages of spreadsheet modeling, the ability to duplicate calculations without having to start over again).
9. The next variable you need to insert in the appropriate cell in the spreadsheet is *Total Receipt*.
10. Select the cell in which you want to place "Total Receipt" as a subheading (i.e., B10).
11. Select the cell in which you want to place the **total receipt formula** (i.e., E10).
12. Type an equal sign (=) to start the formula. Since you are adding more than two variables, you could use the sum function to make it faster. Hence, type in SUM after the equal sign (=) followed with an open parenthesis to form [=SUM ( ]. Select the cells you want to sum up in the formula (i.e., E7:E9). When you select the cells, a border surrounds the cells indicating the cell you are summing up, which will appear on the formula bar. Next, insert the close parenthesis to form [=SUM (E7:E9)], then press the enter key. Excel calculates the result and displays it in the cell as **$81,869.70**.

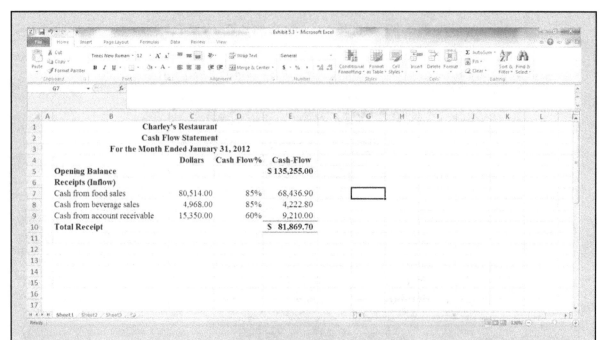

13. The next variable you need to insert in the appropriate spreadsheet cell is *Disbursement*.

14. Select the cell in which you want to place the "Disbursement" subheading (i.e., B11).

15. Identify all the disbursements, list each of them per cell below the "Disbursement" subheading, and insert the appropriate dollar value for each variable in the appropriate cell under the *Dollars* headings. Similarly, insert the appropriate cash flow percentage in the appropriate cell under *Cash Flow %*.

16. Then, compute the cash outflow by multiplying the dollar value of each disbursement by its cash outflow percentage.

> Cash Outflow = Dollars × Cash Outflow Percentage

17. To compute the cash outflow for food cost, select the cell in which you want to place the **cash outflow for food cost formula** (i.e., E12).

18. Type an equal sign (=) to start the formula. Click the first cell you want to place in the formula (i.e., C12). When you click the cell, a border surrounds the cell indicating the cell you are working with and its name appears on the formula bar. Next, type the asterisk (*) key to the formula bar to form [=C12*]. Click the second cell you want to place in the formula (i.e., D12) to form [=C12*D12], then press the enter key. Excel calculates the result and displays it in the cell as **$5,474.95**.

19. At this point of the calculation, you could copy cell E12 and paste it to E13 through E21 to compute a similar calculation for each of the other disbursement variables (or repeat steps 17 and 18 for each of them). If you copy and paste correctly, *beverage cost, operating supplies*, and *accounts payable* due in December will be **$1,207.22 (E13), $8548.20 (E16), and $20,400 (E21)**, respectively (copying and pasting like this is one of the advantages of spreadsheet modeling, the ability to duplicate calculations without having to start over again).

20. The next variable you need to insert in the appropriate cell in the spreadsheet is *Total Disbursement*.

21. Select the cell in which you want to place "Total Disbursement" as the subheading (i.e., B22).

22. Select the cell in which you want to place the **total disbursement formula** (i.e., E22).

23. Type an equal sign (=) to start the formula. Since you are adding more than two variables, you could use the sum function to make it faster. Hence, type in SUM after the equal sign (=) followed with an open parenthesis to form [=SUM ( ]. Select the cells you want to sum up in the formula (i.e., E12:E21). When you select the cells, a border surrounds the cells indicating the cell you are summing up, which will appear on the formula bar. Next, insert the close parenthesis to form [=SUM (E12:E21)], then press the enter key. Excel calculates the result and displays it in the cell as **$71,532.82**.

24. The next variable you need to insert in the appropriate spreadsheet cell is *Net Cash Flow*, also referred to as closing bank balance.

25. Select the cell in which you want to place "Net Cash Flow" as the subheading (i.e., B23).

> Net Cash Flow = Opening Balance + Total Receipt – Total Disbursement

26. Select the cell in which you want to place the **net cash flow formula** (i.e., E23).

27. Type an equal sign (=) to start the formula. Click the first cell you want to place in the formula (i.e., E5). When you click the cell, a border surrounds the cell indicating the cell you are working with and its name appears on the formula bar. Next, type the plus (+) key to the formula bar to form [=E5+]. Click the second cell you want to place in the formula (i.e., E10) to form [=E5+E10]. Next, type the minus (-) key to the formula bar to form [=E5+E10-]. Click the third cell you want to place in the formula (i.e., E22) to form [=E5+E10-E22], then press the enter key. Excel calculates the result and displays it in the cell as **$145,591.88**.

Exhibit 5.3: Spreadsheet-Modeling Approach to Example 5.2

The answer to Example 5.2 using the spreadsheet-modeling approach is displayed in Exhibit 5.3. If your spreadsheet answers are different from the answers as shown in Exhibit 5.3, do not despair. Just locate your mistake and correct the specific cell(s).

ACCOUNTING AND FINANCIAL TERMINOLOGY

Accounts payable *are the amounts a business entity owes for items or services purchased on credit without a promissory note that needs to be paid within a year.*

Accounts receivable *is the value of the money that is yet to be collected for providing products and/or services to customers.*

Balance sheet *is a financial report that shows the net worth of an organization in the form of assets, liabilities, and owner equity at a specific point in time.*

Cash flow *is a term describing cash receipts (inflows) and cash payments or disbursements (outflows).*

Cash flow statement *is a financial report that shows how much cash is generated, used, and retained by an organization in a specific period.*

Cash inflow *is the cash received by a business entity for products or services sold (e.g., the cash received for food and beverage sales).*

Cash outflow *is the cash paid by a business entity to suppliers for inventories and operating expenses (e.g., the cash paid for food and beverage cost).*

Current assets *are cash and other assets that can be converted into cash within one year (e.g., cash, accounts receivable, inventories, etc.).*

Current liabilities *are debts and other obligations that are less than one year (e.g., accounts payable, tax payable, accrued expenses, etc.).*

Long-term debts *are liabilities and other obligations of a business entity longer than a one-year obligation (e.g., mortgage loans, lease obligations, etc.).*

Net cash flow (closing bank balance) *is the amount left in the bank account of the business entity after balancing the cash flow statement.*

Owner's equity *refers to the owner's claim of the resources with economic value, which are expected to provide benefits to future operations*

Summary

The preparation of the balance sheet starts with the ability to identify and separate assets from liabilities. Compute the total assets and the total liabilities followed by the calculation of the owner's equity. The owner's equity is the difference between total assets and total liabilities. The next variable after owner's equity in the balance sheet is the liabilities and owner's equity, which is equal to the assets. Hence, Assets = Liabilities + Owner's Equity.

The preparation of the cash flow statement starts with the ability to identify opening balance and identify and separate receipts from disbursements. Compute the total receipt and the total disbursement followed by calculation of net cash flow. The net cash flow is the addition of the opening balance and total receipt minus total disbursements. Hence, Net Cash Flow = Opening Balance + Total Receipts − Total Disbursement.

Keywords and Concepts

Accounts Payable	Cash Outflow
Accounts Receivable	Current Assets
Balance Sheet	Current Liabilities
Cash Flow	Long-Term Debts
Cash Flow Statement	Net Cash Flow (Closing Bank Balance)
Cash Inflow	Owner's Equity

Review Questions

1. **Scenario:** The following data is adapted from the February 2012 financial record of Charley's Restaurant.

Variables	Dollars
Cash in bank	10,000.00
Accounts receivable	20,250.00
Inventories	15,300.80
Accounts payable	25,255.50
Prepaid rent	3,000.00
Accrued property tax	15,600.60
Prepaid advertising	1000.00
Prepaid insurance	2,250.00
Advance payment	7,500.00
Accrued utilities	6,000.50
Furniture and equipment	45,300.00
Operating equipment	5,500.50
Accumulated depreciation	-1,500.00
Accrued payroll	20,250.75
Long-term debt	25,000.00
Accrued credit card commission	2,500.25

Question: If you are the restaurant manager of Charley's Restaurant, solve the following:

I. Arrange the given information into assets and liabilities.
II. Use the spreadsheet-modeling approach to prepare a balance sheet for the month of February, computing the total assets, total current liability, total liability, owner's equity, and total liability and owner's equity of the business to date.
   a. What is Charley's Restaurant's total assets?
   b. What is Charley's Restaurant's total current liability?
   c. What is Charley's Restaurant's total liability?
   d. What is Charley's Restaurant's owner's equity?
   e. What is Charley's Restaurant's total liabilities and owner's equity?

2. **Scenario:** During the month ended February 29, 2012, Paradise Restaurant had the following income and expense information:

Variable	Dollars
Food revenue	$100,550.00
Beverage revenue	5,900.00
Food cost	32,370.75
Beverage cost	2,100.00
Payroll and related expenses	28,500.00
Employee meals	1,500.00
Operating supplies	9,500.20
Administration and general	1,500.25
Advertising and promotion	2,500.00
Repairs and maintenance	1,250.00
Energy cost	4,100.25

Question: As the restaurant manager of Paradise Restaurant, in addition to the above information you are informed that the cash sales percentages are 75 for food and 75 for beverage. Ninety percent of the $25,550 credit sales in Paradise Restaurant's January accounts receivable were collected. Twenty-five percent of the January cost of food and 95 percent of the cost of beverage were paid in cash, 100 percent of all operating expenses were paid in cash, and 80 percent of accounts payable for January's $15,500 F&B purchases were paid in February. Solve the following:

I. Arrange the given information into receipts and disbursements.
II. Use the spreadsheet-modeling approach to prepare a cash flow statement for the month ended February 29, computing the total receipts, total disbursements, and net cash flow (closing bank balance) of the business to date. The opening cash balance on February 1 was $19,502.

CHAPTER SIX

Budgeting

Learning Objectives

After studying this chapter, you should be able to:

1. Describe different types of budgets.
2. Describe revenue and expense.
3. Describe budget preparation steps.
4. Demonstrate the use of the spreadsheet-modeling approach for budget preparation.

Budgets

Budgets are plans for operating an organization stated in financial terminologies. Budget is also referred to as a projection of an entity's revenue and expenses over a specified future period of time. A budget can be made for a person, family, association, event, business, or government. **Budgeting** is the process of planning and preparing a budget to influence profit in relation to revenue and expenses. Budgeting provides an objective plan in numerical terms for controlling the operations of an organization. Controlling is an important management function for ensuring that plans are being followed. Therefore, the importance of knowing and understanding budgets and budgeting concepts by a manager cannot be overly emphasized.

Advantages of Budgeting and Budgetary Control

There are a number of advantages to budgeting and budgetary control:

- Influence management to look ahead and make plans for achieving the organization's goal/objective.
- Influences each department manager to anticipate plans to give the organization a direction.

- Clarify the areas of responsibility for each department or unit manager for the achievement of budget targets for the operations under her or his personal control.
- Promote efficient organization and communication within and between departments.
- Provide a basis for the organization's performance appraisal by comparing and contrasting the organization's actual performance results against budgeted plans.
- Facilitate the allocation of scarce resources.

Types of Budgets

There are several types of budgets; however, three popular budgets common to all hospitality businesses, as well as other business organizations, are the capital budget, cash budget, and annual operating budget. The following paragraphs will focus on these three different types of budgets.

Capital Budgets

Capital budgets are the projected amount planned to be used for capital items in a given period. Capital items are fixed assets such as equipment and facility renovation or expansion, the cost of which is normally written off over a period of time. Capital budgeting is a long-term economic or investment decision. Hence, it is called a capital budget. The potential project's value (in terms of cash inflows and outflows) is usually assessed using performance measurements such as **internal rate of return**, **net present value**, and **payback period** in relation to the capital item or project. A potential project's lifetime cash inflows and outflows are usually assessed to determine whether the potential returns from the projects are worth the investment.

Cash Budgets

Cash budgets as initially defined in Chapter 3 are forecasts of the cash inflows and outflows expectations for a specific accounting period. The ability to forecast the future cash inflows and outflows requires management's splendid understanding of the organization's operations and other financial activities. Cash budgets are similar to the cash flow statement in that both financial reports show the organization's cash receipts and disbursements (payments) for a specific period. Some of their differences, however, are shown below:

Cash Flow Statement	Cash Budget
• Indicates the real cash flow results of the past period.	A forecast of the cash flow results of the future period.
• Financial statement for stakeholders outside the organization.	Budget used by stakeholders (management) within the organization.

Management can use cash budgets to plan its monthly operations and compare and contrast past operations as needed. Managers who are interested in profitable operations with adequate cash flow are urged to utilize cash budgets. For example, without utilizing a cash budget, offering bottled water at a cost of one dollar ($1) a day to your first twenty customers on a regular basis seems reasonable. A cash budget, however, will indicate that this apparently small daily gesture comes out to an annual total of $7,300 ($1 × 20 × 365 days), which could negatively affect the liquidity of some businesses.

Annual Operating Budgets

Annual operating budgets are thorough projections of revenue and expenses based on a rationally forecasted sale of products and/or services during a specified period (usually one year). The annual operating budget usually contains the organization's revenue goal or what each department in the organization is projected to attain in the upcoming year. It also contains the cost/expense amounts the organization intends to spend to attain the budgeted revenue, profits, and cash flow of the budget duration. Some of the characteristics of annual operating budgets are as follows:

1. It is a plan for the next fiscal year.
2. It is mostly based on the previous year's actual financial results.
3. It usually considers the organization's strengths, weaknesses, opportunities, and threats (SWOT) analysis over the previous year.
4. The preparation and presentation of the budget usually includes a dollar amount and the corresponding percentage for each variable or items listed in the budget.
5. The preparation of the budget usually starts with projected revenue (termed the "head" of the budget) and ends with net income before or after tax.

In the lodging industry, annual operating budgets are prepared for each department in the hotel or resort to include the specifics of each department for the fiscal year. All of the department's annual operating budgets are combined to make the **consolidated budget** or total hotel or resort budget.

Consolidated Budget

The consolidated budget summarizes all the projected revenues, expenses, and net income of the organization for the specified fiscal year. Its main purpose is to display the overall projected revenue and/or expenses for each department in the hotel, and to present the potential financial results for all of the hotel departments combined.

Impact of Revenue and Expenses on Budget

In the hospitality industry and other business organizations, management's goal is to have a situation in which the revenue exceeds the expenses. When the revenue exceeds the expenses, this is referred to as profit in business; government refers to it as budget surplus, and a person or family refers to it as savings.

There is another budget situation in which the revenue equals expenses. When the revenue equals expenses, this is referred to as a breakeven in business; government refers to it as a balanced budget, and a person or family could also refer to it as a breakeven situation.

It is not uncommon for some entities to experience a situation in which the expenses exceed the revenue. When this occurs it is referred to as loss in business; government refers to it as a budget deficit, and for a person or family this is the time when they turn to credit cards or other forms of loans due to overspending.

Bearing the above in mind, it is obvious that managers need to be able to rationally estimate the appropriate revenue for the specified period of a budget, which is mainly the ability to come up with a realistic sales forecast to offset the estimated expenses.

Budget Preparation Steps

The first step in the preparation of a budget is to determine a projected revenue (termed "head" of the budget) since it is usually the first item on top of the budget. Determining the revenue requires a realistic sales forecast of the products/services provided by the organization. **Forecasting** is the ability to use past data to estimate future events. Most forecasts are based on intuition and any of the following methods:

- The inputs from historical data
- Market research
- Statistical methods
- Mathematical models
- Sales department opinion

In addition to the above methods, management should also consider the following conditions for a realistic forecast:

- Economic and political conditions and trends of the region
- Changes in population
- The scope of competition
- The organization's sales and marketing campaign plans
- Consumers' income and interest in the organizations product/services

In the hospitality industry, adequate historical data constitute the most popular forecasting method. In the restaurant business, past customer counts, sales records, and average customer expenditure are used for sales forecast. Similarly, in the lodging industry, the number of rooms sold and the average daily rate are used for sales forecast. As such, revenue in the restaurant and lodging businesses are based on the following formulas as outlined in Chapter 1:

Formulas

6.1. Revenue = Average Customer Expenditure (ACE) × Number of Customers Served

6.2. Revenue = Average Daily Rate (ADR) × Number of Rooms Sold

6.3. $\text{ADR} = \dfrac{\text{Total Room Revenue}}{\text{Total Number of Rooms Sold}}$

6.4. $\text{RevPAR} = \dfrac{\text{Total Room Revenue}}{\text{Total Number of Rooms Available}}$

6.5. Total Rooms Sold = Occupancy Rate × Total Number of Rooms Available

The formulas above for revenue refer to total sales. The revenue formula in 5.1 is used for restaurants, while the revenue formula in 5.2 is mostly used in the lodging (motel and hotel) industry.

The second step in the preparation of a restaurant budget is to determine the potential cost of food and beverage. Although the food and beverage cost is highly affected by management's choice of food and beverage purveyors, the food and beverage cost forecast is based on historical data in relation to estimated percentages of food and beverage sales, respectively.

The third step in preparation of a restaurant budget is to determine gross profit. This aspect of the budget is basically an arithmetic calculation, which is the difference between revenue and the cost of goods sold (cost of sales). The cost of sales is the combination of the food cost and beverage cost.

The fourth step in preparation of a restaurant budget is to determine **operating expenses,** which are the costs of the goods and services utilized to earn revenue (sales). Some examples of operating expenses as outlined in Chapter 4 include payroll and related expenses, cost of supplies, advertising and promotion, repairs and maintenance, energy cost, etc. The operating expenses can be classified into fixed and variable costs. The variable costs are mostly based on historical data in relation to estimated percentages of the cost of sales.

The fifth step in preparation of a restaurant budget is to determine the **net profit before tax** as described in Chapter 1 (Formula 1.2), which is the total sales (revenue) minus the cost of goods sold (COGS) and all other operating expenses except taxes.

The sixth step in preparation of a restaurant budget is to determine the **net profit after tax** as described in Chapter 1 (Formula 1.3), which is the total sale (revenue) minus the cost of goods sold (COGS), and all other operating expenses and taxes. It is also known as earnings after tax, net income after tax, or net income. Now that you are familiar with the preparation of an operating budget, the following example will illustrate the preparation of an annual operating budget using a spreadsheet-modeling approach.

Spreadsheet-Modeling Approach for Annual Operating Budget Preparation

EXAMPLE 6.1

Scenario: A 300-room hotel located in St. Charles operates a restaurant called Charley's Kitchen. As a manager of the restaurant you must prepare next year's budget for your department. After receiving information about last year's budget (see Exhibit 6.1) from your general manager, you are ready to prepare a budget for the next fiscal year.

Exhibit 6.1: The restaurant's (Charley's Kitchen) 2012 budget (last year's)

Variables	Fiscal Year 2012	
Sales	**Dollars**	**Percentage**
Food	$ 1,225,000.00	94.22%
Beverage	75,200.00	5.78%
Total Sales	**1,300,200.00**	**100.00%**
Cost of Sales		
Food	392,000.00	32.00%
Beverage	21,056.00	28.00%
Total Cost of Sales	**413,056.00**	**31.77%**
Total Gross Profit	**887,144.00**	**68.23%**
Operating Expenses		
Payroll and related expenses	351,054.00	27.00%
Employee meals	15,602.40	1.20%
Operating supplies	105,316.20	8.10%
Administration and general	22,753.50	1.75%
Advertising and promotion	22,103.40	1.70%
Repairs and maintenance	14,952.30	1.15%
Energy cost	43,556.70	3.35%
Total Operating Expenses	**575,338.50**	**44.25%**
Net Income Before Tax	$ **311,805.50**	**23.98%**

After careful analyses of past records, local markets, and competition, you decide on the following to improve Charley's Kitchen's budget for the next fiscal year:

I. Allocate an additional $3,500 per month to advertising and promotion.
II. Increase food sales by 20 percent.
III. Increase beverage sales by 30 percent.
IV. Lower food cost percentage from 32 percent to 28 percent.
V. Lower beverage cost percentage from 28 percent to 25 percent.
VI. Increase operating supplies by $1,000 per month.

VII. Increase energy cost by $500 per month.

VIII. Increase payroll and related expenses by $4,000 per month.

IX. All other operating expense categories remain at the current percentage of revenue.

Questions: Present a budget for the next fiscal year reflecting the changes proposed. If the current tax rate is as shown on the following table, what is the projected net income after tax for next year's budget?

Tax Rate (%)	Income Level
10	$0–$17,900
15	$17,901–$72,500
25	$72,501–$146,400
28	$146,401–$223,050
33	$223,051–$398,350
35	$398,351–$450,000
39.6	Over $450,000

ANSWER: To solve this question, you need to be familiar with some formulas as outlined in (Formulas 5.1–5.5), remember the spreadsheet design guiding principles in Chapter 1, as listed in Exhibit 4.3, then follow the step-by-step, hands-on approach to Example 6.1 as outlined below.

By following these instructions you should be done preparing a budget for FY 2013. If you make any mistakes in typing any of numbers, do not panic. Just make the necessary changes and all the calculations will be automatically corrected. The answer to Example 6.1 using the spreadsheet-modeling approach is displayed in Exhibit 6.2.

STEP-BY-STEP, HANDS-ON APPROACH TO EXAMPLE 6.1

1. In your Excel spreadsheet, start with the headings of the budget by inserting *Variables, Fiscal Year 2012,* and *Fiscal Year 2013* in columns B1, CD1, and EF1, respectively.
2. Following the first set of headings, insert *Sales, Dollars, Percentage, Dollars,* and *Percentage* in columns B2, C2, D2, E2, and F2, respectively.
3. Insert the given variables (food sales, beverage sales, food cost, etc.) under variables and insert the appropriate dollar and percentage values for each variable in the appropriate cell under the *Dollars* and *Percentage* headings, respectively.

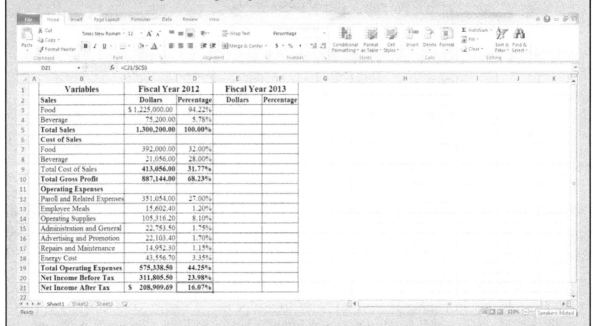

4. The first step is to determine the projected revenue (*Sales,* at "head" of the budget), which is based on a 20 percent increase in Food Sales (FS) and a 30 percent increase in Beverage Sales (BS).
5. Start by computing the fiscal year (FY) 2013 projected FS.

$$20\% \text{ Increase in Food Sales} = \text{FY2012 FS} + (\text{FY2012 FS} \times 20\%)$$
$$= \$1,225,000 + (\$1,225,000 \times 20\%)$$

6. Select the cell in which you want to place the **FS formula** (i.e., E3).
7. Type an equal sign (=) to start the formula. Click the first cell you want to place in the formula (i.e., C3). When you click the cell, a border surrounds the cell indicating the cell you are working with and its name appears on the formula bar. Next, type the plus (+) key to the formula bar to form [=C3+]. Click the open parenthesis key to the formula bar to form [=C3+ ( ]. Click the second cell you want to place in the formula (i.e., C3) to form [=C3+ (C3], then press the asterisk (*) key to form [=C3+ (C3*]. Type in the percentage increase (20%) to form [=C3+ (C3*20%]. Click the close parenthesis key to the formula bar to form [=C3+ (C3*20%)], then press the enter key. Excel calculates the result and displays it in the cell as **$1,470,000.**

8. The next variable to compute is *BS*. Start by selecting the cell in which you want to place the **BS formula** (i.e., E4).

9. Type an equal sign (=) to start the formula. Click the first cell you want to place in the formula (i.e., C4). When you click the cell, a border surrounds the cell indicating the cell you are working with and its name appears on the formula bar. Next, type the plus (+) key to the formula bar to form [=C4+]. Click the open parenthesis key to the formula bar to form [=C4+ ( ]. Click the second cell you want to place in the formula (i.e., C4) to form [=C4+ (C4], then press the asterisk (*) key to form [=C4+ (C4*]. Type in the percentage increase (20%) to form [=C4+ (C4*20%]. Click the close parenthesis key to the formula bar to form [=C4+ (C4*20%)], then press the enter key. Excel calculates the result and displays it in the cell as **$97,760**.

10. The next variable to compute is *Total Sales*. Start by selecting the cell in which you want to place the **total sales formula** (i.e., E5)

11. Type an equal sign (=) to start the formula. Click the first cell you want to place in the formula (i.e., E3). When you click the cell, a border surrounds the cell indicating the cell you are working with and its name appears on the formula bar. Next, type the plus (+) key to the formula bar to form [=E3+]. Click the second cell you want to place in the formula (i.e., E4) to form [=E3+E4], then press the enter key. Excel calculates the result and displays it in the cell as **$1,567,760**.

12. The next variables to compute are *Cost of Sales*.

13. Start by selecting the cell in which you want to place the **Food Cost (FC) formula** (i.e., E7)

> Decrease Food Cost to 28% = FY2013 FS × 28%
> = $1,470,000 × 28%

14. Type an equal sign (=) to start the formula. Click the first cell you want to place in the formula (i.e., E3). When you click the cell, a border surrounds the cell indicating the cell you are working with and its name appears on the formula bar. Next, click the asterisk (*) key to the formula bar to form [=E3*] Type in the appropriate percentage (28%) to form [=E3*28%], then press the enter key. Excel calculates the result and displays it in the cell as **$411,600**.

15. The next variable to compute is *Beverage Cost* (BC). Start by selecting the cell in which you want to place the **BC formula** (i.e., E8).

16. Type an equal sign (=) to start the formula. Click the first cell you want to place in the formula (i.e., E4). When you click the cell, a border surrounds the cell indicating the cell you are working with and its name appears on the formula bar. Next, click the asterisk (*) key to the formula bar to form [=E4*]. Type in the appropriate percentage (25%) to form [=E4*25%], then press the enter key. Excel calculates the result and displays it in the cell as **$24,440**.

17. The next variable to compute is *Total Cost of Sales*. Start by selecting the cell in which you want to place the **total cost of sales formula** (i.e., E9).

18. Type an equal sign (=) to start the formula. Click the first cell you want to place in the formula (i.e., E7). When you click the cell, a border surrounds the cell indicating the cell you are working with and its name appears on the formula bar. Next, type the plus (+) key to the formula bar to form [=E7+]. Click the second cell you want to place in the formula (i.e., E8) to form [=E7+E8], then press the enter key. Excel calculates the result and displays it in the cell as **$436,040**.

19. The next variable you need to insert in the appropriate cell in the spreadsheet is *Gross Profit*.

> Gross profit = Total Sales – Total Cost of Sales

20. Select the cell in which you want to place the **gross profit formula** (i.e., E10)
21. Type an equal sign (=) to start the formula. Click the first cell you want to place in the formula (i.e., E5). When you click the cell, a border surrounds the cell indicating the cell you are working with and its name appears on the formula bar. Next, type the minus (–) key to the formula bar to form [=E5–]. Click the second cell you want to place in the formula (i.e., E9) to form [=E5–E9], then press the enter key. Excel calculates the result and displays it in the cell as **$1,131,720**.
22. The next variables to compute are *Operating Expenses*. Start by selecting the cell in which you want to place the **payroll and related expenses formula** (i.e., E12).
23. Since the plan is to increase last year's payroll and related expenses by $4,000 per month, the formula will be last year's payroll and related expenses plus ($4,000 × 12).
24. Type an equal sign (=) to start the formula. Click the first cell you want to place in the formula (i.e., C12). When you click the cell, a border surrounds the cell indicating the cell you are working with and its name appears on the formula bar. Next, type the plus (+) key to the formula bar to form [=C12+]. Click the open parenthesis key to the formula bar to form [=C12+ ( ]. Type in 4000 to form [=C12+ (4000], then press the asterisk (*) key to form [=C12+ (4000*]. Type in 12 (for twelve months) to form [=C12+ (4000*12]. Click the close parenthesis key to the formula bar to form [=C12+ (4000*12)], then press the enter key. Excel calculates the result and displays it in the cell as **$399,054**.
25. The next variable to compute is *Employee Meals*. It is one of the variables that remain at the current percentage of revenue. Hence, just multiply the percentage by the new FY's revenue (total sales).
26. Select the cell in which you want to place the **employee meals formula** (i.e., E13).
27. Type an equal sign (=) to start the formula. Click the first cell you want to place in the formula (i.e., E5). When you click the cell, a border surrounds the cell indicating the cell you are working with and its name appears on the formula bar. Next, click the asterisk (*) key to the formula bar to form [=E5*]. Type in the appropriate percentage (1.20%) to form [=E5*1.20%], then press the enter key. Excel calculates the result and displays it in the cell as **$18,813.12**.
28. The next variable to compute is *Operating Supplies*. Since the plan is to increase last year's operating supplies expenses by $1,000 per month, the formula will be last year's operating supplies expenses plus ($1,000 × 12).
29. Select the cell in which you want to place the **operating supplies formula** (i.e., E14).
30. Type an equal sign (=) to start the formula. Click the first cell you want to place in the formula (i.e., C14). When you click the cell, a border surrounds the cell indicating the cell you are working with and its name appears on the formula bar. Next, type the plus (+) key to the formula bar to form [=C14+]. Click the open parenthesis key to the formula bar to form [=C14+ ( ]. Type in 1000 to form [=C14+ (1000], then press the asterisk (*) key to form [=C14+ (1000*]. Type in 12 (for twelve months) to form [=C14+ (1000*12]. Click the close parenthesis key to the formula bar to form [=C14+ (1000*12)], then press the enter key. Excel calculates the result and displays it in the cell as **$117,316.20**.

31. The next variable to compute is *Administration and General* expense. It is one of the variables that remain at the current percentage of revenue. Hence, just multiply the percentage by the new FY's revenue (total sales).

32. Select the cell in which you want to place the **administration and general expense formula** (i.e., E15).

33. Type an equal sign (=) to start the formula. Click the first cell you want to place in the formula (i.e., E5). When you click the cell, a border surrounds the cell indicating the cell you are working with and its name appears on the formula bar. Next, click the asterisk (*) key to the formula bar to form [=E5*]. Type in the appropriate percentage (1.75%) to form [=E5*1.75%], then press the enter key. Excel calculates the result and displays it in the cell a **$27,435.80**.

34. The next variable to compute is the *Advertising and Promotion* expense. Since the plan is to increase last year's advertising and promotion expenses by $3,500 per month, the formula will be last year's advertising and promotion expenses plus ($3,500 × 12).

35. Select the cell in which you want to place the **advertising and promotion formula** (i.e., E16).

36. Type an equal sign (=) to start the formula. Click the first cell you want to place in the formula (i.e., C16). When you click the cell, a border surrounds the cell indicating the cell you are working with and its name appears on the formula bar. Next, type the plus (+) key to the formula bar to form [=C16+]. Click the open parenthesis key to the formula bar to form [=C16+ ( ]. Type in 3500 to form [=C16+ (3500], then press the asterisk (*) key to form [=C16+ (3500*]. Type in 12 (for twelve months) to form [=C16+ (3500*12]. Click the close parenthesis key to the formula bar to form [=C16+ (3500*12)], then press the enter key. Excel calculates the result and displays it in the cell as **$64,103.40**.

37. The next variable to compute is the *Repair and Maintenance* expense. It is one of the variables that remain at the current percentage of revenue. Hence, just multiply the percentage by the new FY's revenue (total sales).

38. Select the cell in which you want to place the **repair and maintenance expense formula** (i.e., E17).

39. Type an equal sign (=) to start the formula. Click the first cell you want to place in the formula (i.e., E5). When you click the cell, a border surrounds the cell indicating the cell you are working with and its name appears on the formula bar. Next, click the asterisk (*) key to the formula bar to form [=E5*] Type in the appropriate percentage (1.75%) to form [=E5*1.15%], then press the enter key. Excel calculates the result and displays it in the cell as **$18,029.24**.

40. The next variable to compute is *Energy Cost*. Since the plan is to increase last year's energy cost by $500 per month, the formula will be last year's energy cost plus ($500 × 12).

41. Select the cell in which you want to place the **energy cost formula** (i.e., E18).

42. Type an equal sign (=) to start the formula. Click the first cell you want to place in the formula (i.e., C18). When you click the cell, a border surrounds the cell indicating the cell you are working with and its name appears on the formula bar. Next, type the plus (+) key to the formula bar to form [=C18+]. Click the open parenthesis key to the formula bar to form [=C18+ ( ]. Type in 500 to form [=C18+ (500], then press the asterisk (*) key to form [=C18+ (500*]. Type in 12 (for twelve months) to form [=C18+ (500*12]. Click the close parenthesis key to the formula bar to form [=C18+ (500*12)], then press the enter key. Excel calculates the result and displays it in the cell as **$49,556.70**.

43. The next variable to compute is *Total Operating Expenses*.

> **Total Operating Expenses = The Sum of All the Operating Expenses**

44. Select the cell in which you want to place the **total operating expenses formula** (i.e., E19)
45. Type an equal sign (=) to start the formula. Since you are adding more than two variables, you could use the sum function to make it faster. Hence, type in SUM after the equal sign (=) followed with an open parenthesis to form [=SUM ( ]. Select the cells you want to sum up in the formula (i.e., E12:E18). When you select the cells, a border surrounds the cells indicating the cell you are summing up, which will appear on the formula bar. Next, insert the close parenthesis to form [=SUM (E12:E18)], then press the enter key. Excel calculates the result and displays it in the cell as **$694,308.46**.
46. The next variable you need to insert in the appropriate cell in the spreadsheet is *Net Income Before Tax* (NIBT).

> **Net Income Before Tax = Gross Profit – Total Operating Expenses**

47. Select the cell in which you want to place the **NIBT formula** (i.e., E20)
48. Type an equal sign (=) to start the formula. Click the first cell you want to place in the formula (i.e., E10). When you click the cell, a border surrounds the cell indicating the cell you are working with and its name appears on the formula bar. Next, type the minus (–) key to the formula bar to form [=E10 –]. Click the second cell you want to place in the formula (i.e., E19) to form [=E10-E19], then press the enter key. Excel calculates the result and displays it in the cell as **$437,411.54**.
49. The next variable you need to insert in the appropriate cell in the spreadsheet is *Net Income After Tax*.

> **Net Income After Tax = NIBT – (NIBT × Appropriate Tax Rate)**

50. Select the cell in which you want to place the **net income after tax formula** (i.e., E21).
51. Type an equal sign (=) to start the formula. Click the first cell you want to place in the formula (i.e., E20). When you click the cell, a border surrounds the cell indicating the cell you are working with and its name appears on the formula bar. Next, type the minus (–) key to the formula bar to form [=E20 –]. Click the open parenthesis key to the formula bar to form [=E20 – ( ]. Click the second cell you want to place in the formula (i.e., E20) to form [=E20 – (E20], then press the asterisk (*) key to form [=E20 –(E20*]. Type in the appropriate tax rate (i.e., 35%) to form [=E20 – (E20*35%]. Click the close parenthesis key to the formula bar to form [=E20 –(E20*35%)], then press the enter key. Excel calculates the result and displays it in the cell as **$284,317.50**.
52. Now that you are done calculating all the necessary variables in the *Dollars* column, it is time to calculate the percentages for each variable.
53. Let us start with the *Food Sales Percentage*.

> $$\text{Food Sales Percentage} = \frac{\text{Food Sales}}{\text{Total Sales (Revenue)}}$$

54. Select the cell in which you want to place the **food sales percentage formula** (i.e., F3).

55. Type an equal sign (=) to start the formula. Click the first cell you want to place in the formula (i.e., E3). When you click the cell, a border surrounds the cell indicating the cell you are working with and its name appears on the formula bar. Next, type the slash (/) key to the formula bar to form [=E3/]. Click the second cell you want to place in the formula (i.e., E5) to form [=E3/E5]. To make this formula applicable to more cells, insert the dollar sign ($) in front of the E and 5 of E5 to form [=E3/$E$5], then press the enter key. Excel calculates the result and displays it in the cell as **0.9376**.

56. Since this is supposed to be in percentage, click the percentage (%) sign in the Excel tool bar. Excel calculates the result and displays it in the cell. If you limit your result to two decimal places you will have **93.76%**.

57. To calculate the rest of the percentages, just copy the cell F3 (93.76%) and paste it into any of the cells you want to calculate except when calculating for food cost and beverage cost percentages.

58. To calculate the *Food Cost Percentage* use the formula below (4.6).

$$\text{Food Cost Percentage} = \frac{\text{Food Cost}}{\text{Food Sales}}$$

59. Select the cell in which you want to place the **food cost percentage formula** (i.e., F7).

60. Type an equal sign (=) to start the formula. Click the first cell you want to place in the formula (i.e., E7). When you click the cell, a border surrounds the cell indicating the cell you are working with and its name appears on the formula bar. Next, type the slash (/) key to the formula bar to form [=E7/]. Click the second cell you want to place in the formula (i.e., E3) to form [=E7/E3], then press the enter key. Excel calculates the result and displays it in the cell as **0.2800**.

61. Click the percentage (%) sign in the Excel tool bar. Excel calculates the result and displays it in the cell. If you limit your result to two decimal places you will have **28.00%**.

62. To calculate the *Beverage Cost Percentage* use the formula below (4.7).

$$\text{Beverage Cost Percentage} = \frac{\text{Beverage Cost}}{\text{Beverage Sales}}$$

63. Select the cell in which you want to place the **beverage cost percentage formula** (i.e., F8).

64. Type an equal sign (=) to start the formula. Click the first cell you want to place in the formula (i.e., E8). When you click the cell, a border surrounds the cell indicating the cell you are working with and its name appears on the formula bar. Next, type the slash (/) key to the formula bar to form [=E8/]. Click the second cell you want to place in the formula (i.e., E4) to form [=E8/E4], then press the enter key. Excel calculates the result and displays it in the cell as **0.2500**.

65. Click the percentage (%) sign in the Excel tool bar. Excel calculates the result and displays it in the cell. If you limit your result to two decimal places you will have **25.00%**.

66. Again, to calculate the rest of the percentages, just copy the cell F3 (93.76%) and paste it into any of the cells you want to calculate except when calculating for food cost and beverage cost percentages.

Exhibit 6.2: Spreadsheet-Modeling Approach to Example 6.1

Variables	Fiscal Year 2012		Fiscal Year 2013	
	Dollars	Percentage	Dollars	Percentage
Sales				
Food	$ 1,225,000.00	94.22%	$ 1,470,000.00	93.76%
Beverage	75,200.00	5.78%	97,760.00	6.24%
Total Sales	**1,300,200.00**	**100.00%**	**1,567,760.00**	**100.00%**
Cost of Sales				
Food	392,000.00	32.00%	411,600.00	28.00%
Beverage	21,056.00	28.00%	24,440.00	25.00%
Total Cost of Sales	**413,056.00**	**31.77%**	**436,040.00**	**27.81%**
Total Gross Profit	**887,144.00**	**68.23%**	**1,131,720.00**	**72.19%**
Operating Expenses				
Paroll and Related Expenses	351,054.00	27.00%	399,054.00	25.45%
Employee Meals	15,602.40	1.20%	18,813.12	1.20%
Operating Supplies	105,316.20	8.10%	117,316.20	7.48%
Administration and General	22,753.50	1.75%	27,435.80	1.75%
Advertising and Promotion	22,103.40	1.70%	64,103.40	4.09%
Repairs and Maintenance	14,952.30	1.15%	18,029.24	1.15%
Energy Cost	43,556.70	3.35%	49,556.70	3.16%
Total Operating Expenses	**575,338.50**	**44.25%**	**694,308.46**	**44.29%**
Net Income Before Tax	**311,805.50**	**23.98%**	**437,411.54**	**27.90%**
Net Income After Tax	**$ 208,909.69**	**16.07%**	**$ 284,317.50**	**18.14%**

ACCOUNTING AND FINANCIAL TERMINOLOGY

Annual operating budgets *are thorough projections of revenue and expenses based on a rationally forecasted sale of products and/or services during a specified period (usually one year).*

Budgets *are plans for operating an organization stated in financial terminologies.*

Budgeting *is the process of planning and preparing a budget to influence profit in relation to revenue and expenses.*

Capital budgets *are the projected amount planned to be used for capital items in a given period.*

Cash budgets *are forecasts of the cash inflows and outflows expectations for a specific accounting period.*

Cash flow *is a term describing cash receipts (inflows) and cash payments or disbursements (outflows).*

Cash flow statement *is a financial report that shows how much cash is generated, used, and retained by an organization in a specific period.*

Consolidated budget *summarizes all the projected revenues, expenses, and net income of an organization for the specified fiscal year.*

Cost of sales *is the cost the hospitality establishment paid for the products or the raw materials used to make the products (e.g., food and beverage) that are sold to its customers.*

Fiscal year *is the twelve-month accounting period used by business organizations.*

Gross profit *is the difference between revenue and the cost of goods sold.*

Internal rate of return (IRR) *is an assessment technique used in capital budgeting to analyze the discount rate that makes the net present value of all cash flows from a particular investment or project equal to zero.*

Net cash flow (closing bank balance) *is the amount left in the bank account of the business entity after balancing the cash flow statement.*

Net present value (NPV) *is an assessment technique used in capital budgeting to analyze the difference between the present value of cash inflows and the present value of cash outflows.*

Net profit after tax *is the total sales (revenue) minus the cost of goods sold (COGS) and all other operating expenses and taxes.*

Net profit before tax *is the total sales (revenue) minus the cost of goods sold (COGS) and all other operating expenses except taxes.*

Operating expenses *are the costs of the goods and services utilized to earn revenue (sales).*

Payback period *is the length of time expected to recover the cost of a given investment or project.*

Revenue *is a term that refers to the total sales.*

Summary

A budget is a projection of an entity's revenues and expenses over a specified future period of time. Budgeting provides an objective plan in numerical terms for controlling the operations of an organization. There are several types of budgets, including capital budget, cash budget, and annual operating budget. Budgets could be used to facilitate the allocation of scarce resources and influence management to look ahead and make plans for achieving the organization's goals and objectives.

Preparation of a budget starts with *revenue*, termed the "head" because of its position at the top of the budget. The *revenue* or *total sale* is followed by the *cost of food and beverage sold (cost of sales)*. *Gross profit* follows *cost of sales*, which is the combination of the food cost and beverage cost. Cost of sales is accompanied by *operating expenses, income before tax (net profit before tax)*, and *net profit after tax*, respectively.

When preparing a budget it is very important for the hospitality managers to have the best possible revenue projection. An inappropriate revenue forecast could negatively affect the operation of the business.

Keywords and Concepts

Annual Operating Budgets

Budgets

Budgeting

Capital Budgets

Cash Budgets

Cash Flow

Cash Flow Statement

Consolidated Budget

Cost of Sales

Fiscal Year

Gross Profit

Internal Rate of Return (IRR)

Net Cash Flow (Closing Bank Balance)

Net Present Value (NPV)

Net Profit After Tax

Net Profit Before Tax

Operating Expenses

Payback Period

Revenue

Review Questions

1. **scenario**: Lauren Andrew is a food and beverage manager of a 300-room property near Fayetteville, Arkansas. Lauren was hired because she was a graduate of the hospitality and restaurant management program at the University of Arkansas and had a year of industry experience with a nationwide restaurant chain. She has been empowered to make changes to improve the establishment's bottom line. Last year's (2012) budget for the restaurant showed the following figures:

	FY 2012	
Sales	**Dollars**	**Percentage**
Food	$ 1,050,000.00	92.90%
Beverage	80,200.00	7.10%
Total Sales	**1,130,200.00**	**100.00%**
Cost of Sales		
Food	357,000.00	34.00%
Beverage	21,654.00	27.00%
Total Cost of Sales	378,654.00	33.50%
Total Gross Profit	**751,546.00**	**66.50%**
Operating Expenses		
Payroll and Related Expenses	350,362.00	31.00%
Employee Meals	11,302.00	1.00%
Operating Supplies	107,369.00	9.50%
Administration and general	22,604.00	2.00%

Advertising and promotion	22,604.00	2.00%
Repairs and maintenance	22,604.00	2.00%
Energy Cost	39,557.00	3.50%
Total Operating Expenses	**576,402.00**	**51.00%**
Profit Before Occupancy Costs	**175,144.00**	**15.50%**
Occupancy Costs	56,510.00	5.00%
Income Before Tax	**118,634.00**	**10.50%**
Income After Tax	**$ 88,975.50**	**7.87%**

After careful analyses of past records, local markets, and competition, Lauren decided on the following to improve the establishment's budget for the 2013 fiscal year:

I.   Allocate an additional $2,500 per month to advertising and promotion.
II. Increase food sales by 25 percent.
III. Increase beverage sales by 35 percent.
IV. Lower food cost percentage from 34 percent to 28 percent.
V.   Lower beverage cost percentage from 27 percent to 20 percent.
VI. Increase operating supplies by $1,000 per month.
VII. Increase energy cost by $500 per month.
VIII. Increase payroll and related expenses by $3,000 per month.
IX. Due to city and state regulations, the occupancy cost increased from 5 percent to 5.2 percent.
X.   All other operating expenses categories remain at the current percentage of revenue.

Questions

1. Present a budget for the next fiscal year reflecting the changes proposed by Ms. Andrew.
2. If the current tax rate is as shown on the following table, what is the projected net income after tax for next year's budget?

Tax Rate (%)	Income Level
10	$0–$17,900
15	$17,901–$72,500
25	$72,501–$146,400
28	$146,401–$223,050
33	$223,051–$398,350
35	$398,351–$450,000
39.6	Over $450,000

3. If the predicted cash sales percentages of 60 percent for food and 80 percent for beverage will be received in cash in the next fiscal year's budget:

    a. How much cash will be received from food sales?

    b. How much cash will be received from beverage sales?

4. If 20 percent of the food cost and 85 percent of the cost of beverage will be paid in cash in the next fiscal year's budget:

    a. How much cash will be paid for cost of food sold?

    b. How much cash will be paid for cost of beverage sold?

CHAPTER SEVEN

Revenue Management

Learning Objectives

After studying this chapter, you should be able to:

1. Describe the principles of revenue management
2. Establish rack rate
3. Describe room rate economics
   a. Law of demand and supply
4. Understand the essentials for revenue management
   a. Forecasting occupancy rate
   b. Uses of internal reports (e.g., ADR, RevPAR, occupancy rate, MLOS, CTA, etc.)
   c. Uses of external reports (e.g., occupancy, ADR, and RevPAR indexes, etc.)
   d. Rate and discount management
   e. Revenue management meeting
5. Use the spreadsheet-modeling approach for revenue management

What is Revenue Management

Revenue management (RM) is a tactical approach used to maximize revenues while supplying the same quantity of product. Revenue management may also be referred to as yield management. In most hotels, the hotel revenue manager or the revenue management team is responsible for making the appropriate decisions to maximize revenue. In small hotels, the general manager (GM) is often in charge of revenue management. In mid-size hotels, the front office manager (FOM) and/or the director of sales and marketing (DOSM) or the combination of FOM, DOSM, and GM may serve as a revenue management team. In large and mega hotels, a revenue manager may be hired to serve in this position. Regardless of the size of the hotel, the hotel **revenue manager** or the **revenue management team** refers to individual or individuals who manage the tactics used to maximize revenues. Since the revenue manager and revenue management team are basically the same, for the rest of this chapter both terms will be used interchangeably. The main goal of revenue management is to continuously maximize revenue from a given supply of product. Some examples of industries that use RM are the airline, hotel, vacation, car rental, freight, television ads, and real estate industries. This chapter will focus on the lodging industry's revenue management principles.

Benefits of Revenue Management

Revenue management helps to enhance:

- Forecasting
- Seasonal rack rates and length of stay
- Collaboration and coordination between the revenue management team (e.g., front office, sales divisions, food and beverage manager, revenue manager, general manager, etc.)
- The development of short- and long-term business plans
- Savings in labor costs and other operating expenses
- Revenue and profit maximization

"We estimate that yield management has generated $1.4 billion in incremental revenue in the last 3 years."
R. L. Crandall, chairman and CEO, AMR, 1992

Establishing Rack Rate

Impact of Internal and External Reports

In the lodging industry, when making pricing decisions on room rates, it is very important to consider the impact of internal and/or external reports based on historical data. This is one of the major reasons many lodging establishments use the property management system (PMS), which can be used for various pricing-related functions. Some of the pricing-related functions of PMS include the following:

- To report the overall ADRs for selected historical periods by room type (e.g., double beds [double or queen], kings, and suites).
- To report the overall ADRs for selected historical days (e.g., all past Mondays, Tuesdays, Fridays, or Saturdays).
- To report the overall ADRs for selected historical periods (e.g., last week, last month, last quarter, and last year).

All the above reports are termed **internal reports** because they can all be generated internally with the help of a PMS and adequate historical data. The revenue management team or the management staff (e.g., GM) making the room rate decisions is expected to consider the above reports when making room rate decisions.

Other reports that could be used to make rate decisions are external reports. **External reports** are external performance data on thousands of hotels that could be used to make rate or pricing-related decisions. Some sources of external reports are TravelCLICK and Smith Travel Research (STR), often referred to as a STAR report. The external performance data can be used to provide the following:

- ADR
- RevPAR
- Occupancy percentage

The revenue management team or the management staff (e.g., GM) making the room rate decisions could also utilize the external reports when making these decisions, especially in situations where the internal reports are not available.

Rack Rate

Rack rate is the price per room type at which the lodging establishment sells each room when no discounts are offered to any guest. Rack rates vary per room type. The better or more popular a room is the higher the price (rate). For example, a suite in one hotel will command a higher price than a king or other rooms in the same hotel. Hotel room rates are based on both objective and subjective factors. The ability to express room rates objectively makes it seem more valid, but considerable caution must be undertaken to rationalize the basis for the objective rate establishment. **The Hubbart room rate formula** offers an objective approach to establishing room rates. The Hubbart formula for rate establishment is based on the needs of the organization with an emphasis on the ability to charge a rate worthy of paying all the necessary operating expenses and making a profit for the stakeholders.

The Hubbart Room Rate Formula

To illustrate use of the Hubbart formula, assume an investor has decided to pay $6 million for a 125-room midscale hotel and hopes for a 10 percent return on the investment. If the following situation applies to the investor's hotel:

- Mortgage repayments of $400,000 per year
- Additional fixed costs of $125,000 per year
- 60 percent hotel occupancy rate
- Operational cost of $1,5 million per year
- Desired profit from the food and beverage department of $50,000 per year
- Desired income from telephone charges and all other non-room departments of $10,000

The steps required to compute the potential rate (ADR) using the Hubbart formula is as follows:

1. *Calculate the hotel's target profits.* Multiply the required ROI by the owner's investment:

   $6,000,000 × 10% = **$600,000**

2. *Calculate all fixed expenses.* Include estimates of all fixed costs including leases, interest expenses, mortgages, property taxes, insurance, etc. In this example, the total cost of mortgage and other fixed costs is:

   $400,000 + $125,000 = **$525,000**

3. *Calculate all operational costs.* Include expenses directly and indirectly associated with cleaning and selling rooms, providing food services, and other costs associated with the hotel operation (e.g., franchise fees, human resources, marketing, energy costs, and repair and maintenance). In this example, the operational cost is:

   $1,500,000

4. *Calculate non-rooms income.* Many hotels can make profits from other sources (e.g., spa, golf, food and beverage department, telephone charges, etc.). If these sources generate a loss, the amount of the loss should be used in the calculation. In this example, the profit from non-room departments is:

   $50,000 + $10,000 = **$60,000**

5. *Determine the total room revenue required to meet the hotel's goals and obligations.* The total room revenue is the sum of the operational costs ($1,500,000), hotel's fixed expense ($525,000), and the owner's desired ROI ($600,000). Then deduct the amount of non-room revenue ($60,000). If the non-room revenue was a loss, this loss should be *added*. In this example, the total required room revenue is:

   $1,500,000 + $525,000 + $600,000 − $60,000 = **$2,565,000**

6. *Forecast the number of rooms to be sold based on the estimated occupancy.* Multiply the number of rooms available by the projected occupancy rate. In this example:

   (125 rooms × 365 days) × 60% = **27,375 rooms**

7. *Calculate the hotel's minimum required ADR.* Divide the required room revenue (Step 5) by the number of rooms to be sold (Step 6):

   $2,565,000 ÷ 27,375 = **$93.70**

The Hubbart formula is a useful way to establish a rate because it is objective and it considers the hotel's fixed expense, operational cost, non-room income (or loss), and potential return on investment before determining the minimum room rate required to achieve the investor's goal. There are other ways, however, to determine room rates by utilizing common pricing strategies as described below.

Basic Pricing Strategies

1. **Prestige Pricing:** A hotel sets the rate of its room to be the highest rate in a particular area and justifies the rate with a better product and/or services.

2. ***Follow the Leader Pricing:*** A hotel sets the rate of its room to be the same as its **competitive set** leader in the area. This strategy is made easier with the advent of the Internet (hotel websites), which made it easier to see what the competitors charge.
3. ***Check Around Competitive Pricing:*** A hotel can use websites to select a competitive set of rates to be monitored, check out the real-time room rates offered by these hotels, and determine a competitive rate to charge in relation to the hotel's competitive set. This pricing strategy is gradually replacing the "call around" technique, an inquiry via telephone performed by a hotel staff member to acquire information about other hotels' room rates and availability, which is used by the calling hotel to help determine room rates (Hayes and Ninemeier, 2007). Depending on the hotel's revenue management interest, the rate could be less than, the same as, or more than what the competitors are charging.

All of the above basic pricing strategies are based on the law of supply and demand in relation to consumer behavior. Revenue managers, however, are encouraged to establish room rates by combining consumer behavior, hotel cost structure, and the realities of the economic condition. A pricing strategy that considers all of the above is "Ogbeide's Desired Profit Rate" (ODPR) method.

Ogbeide's Desired Profit Rate (ODPR) Method

The ODPR method can be used by many business organizations to decide on the price (rate) of their product/service to be sold. This method is based on the organizations' desired profit rate and is somewhat similar to the Hubbart formula. But unlike the Hubbart formula, the ODPR could be used to establish the rate of an individual product, such as the rate of a cup of coffee or the average rate of collective products such as the average daily rate of hotel rooms. Another contrast between the ODPR method and the Hubbart formula is that the Hubbart formula is based on return on investment, while the ODPR method is based on the desired profit rate. To illustrate use of the ODPR method, assume a revenue manager in a 125-room midscale hotel hopes for a 20 percent profit before tax in the next fiscal year. If the following situation applies to the hotel, the potential minimum ADR can be computed:

- Fixed expenses (e.g., mortgage repayments, lease, fees, insurance, etc.) = $525,000
- Estimated operational cost based on previous year's = $1,500,000
- Estimated occupancy rate based on internal and external considerations = 60 percent

The steps required to compute the minimum ADR using the ODPR method are as follows:

1. *Calculate all fixed expenses.* Include estimates of all fixed costs including leases, interest expenses, mortgages, property taxes, insurance, etc. In this example, the total fixed expense is **$525,000.**
2. *Calculate all operational costs.* Include expenses directly and indirectly associated the hotel operation (e.g., franchise fees, labor cost, marketing, energy costs, and repair and maintenance). In this example, the operational cost is **$1,500,000.**

3. *Calculate the desired profit.* Many hotels can make profits from other sources (e.g., spa, golf, food and beverage department, telephone charges, etc.). If these sources generate a loss, the amount of the loss should be considered in the calculation. In this example, the desired profit rate is 20 percent. Hence, the desired profit:

$$= \frac{(\text{total expenses} + \text{total operational cost}) \times 20\%}{1-20\%}$$

$$= \frac{(\$525,000 + \$1,500,000) \times 20\%}{80\%} = \frac{(\$525,000 + \$1,500,000) \times 0.20}{0.80}$$

$$= \frac{2,025,000 \times .20}{.80}$$

$$= \mathbf{506,250}$$

4. *Determine the total revenue required to meet the hotel's desired profit.* The total revenue is the sum of the hotel's fixed expense ($525,000), operational costs ($1,500,000), and the desired profit ($506,250). In this example, the total required revenue is:
$1,500,000 + \$525,000 + \$506,250 = \mathbf{\$2,531,250}$

5. *Forecast the number of rooms to be sold based on the estimated occupancy.* Multiply the number of rooms available by the projected occupancy rate. In this example:
(125 rooms × 365 days) × 60% = **27,375 rooms**

6. *Calculate the hotel's minimum required ADR.* Divide the required revenue (Step 4) by the number of rooms to be sold (Step 5):
$2,531,250 ÷ 27,375 = **$92.40**

The ODPR method, like the Hubbart formula, is a useful way to establish rate because it's both objective and also considers the hotel's fixed expense, operational cost, and desired profit before determining the minimum room rate required to achieve the revenue manager's goal. In addition, the ODPR method could also be used by each department in the hotel to set a revenue or profit maximization goal.

Room Rate Economics

Room rate economics refers to how the forces of demand and supply impacts how revenue managers establish room rates to maximize revenue. To utilize room rate economics to maximize revenue, the team or person in charge of revenue management should understand the principle of demand and supply and how it affects room rates. In the lodging industry, **demand** refers to the number of rooms sold while **supply** refers to the number of rooms available for sale. When describing room rate economics, it is very important to understand the fundamental economic law of demand and supply.

The Laws of Demand and Supply

The law of demand states that other things being equal, as price increases, the corresponding quantity demanded decreases. As the price of a product or service decreases, the quantity of that product or service that the market will demand will increase. "Other things equal" here refers to consumer income, tastes, prices of related products or services, and other things beside the price of the product or service being discussed. In contrast, **the law of supply** states that as the price increases for a given product or service, suppliers are willing to supply more. Selling more products or services at a higher price will produce more revenue.

Exhibit 7.1 shows a graphical representation of the laws or demand and supply. The law of demand graph indicates that when the price of a product or service was eighty dollars, only two (2) quantities of the products or services were demanded. When the price of the products or services was reduced to forty dollars, more of the products or services (six quantities) were demanded.

The law of supply graph in Exhibit 7.1 indicates that as the price for a given product or service increases, suppliers are willing to supply more. Hence, when the price of the products or services was eighty dollars, suppliers were willing to sell eight (8) quantities. When the price of the products or services was reduced to forty dollars, a lower amount of the products or services (four quantities) were supplied. Similarly, other things being equal in the lodging industry, the

Exhibit 7.1: The Laws of Demand and Supply

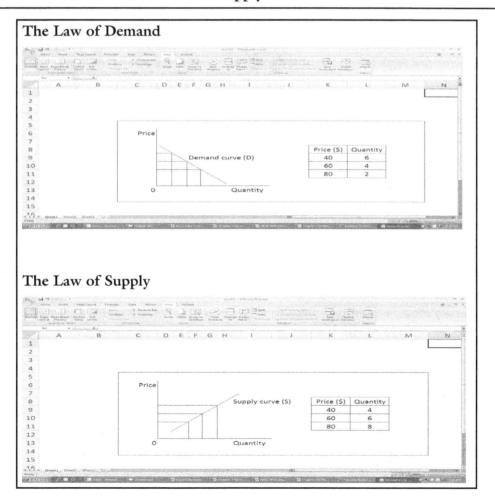

higher the room rates, the more rooms the hoteliers want to supply. The lower the room rates, the more the quantity of rooms demanded by guests.

To illustrate the above laws of demand and supply in the lodging industry, assume that Web City will be the location of an association's annual convention to be held early next year. The convention is supposed to attract enough attendees to sell 65 percent of the rooms available in Web City for the duration of the convention. Consider there are fifty hotels with a total of 10,000 rooms available in Web City for sale. The citywide 65 percent occupancy rate is 6,500 rooms (10,000 rooms × 65%). According to the law of demand, other things being equal, the hotel with the lowest rate would most likely have the highest occupancy rate, and the hotel with the highest rate would most likely have the lowest occupancy rate. What if all 10,000 rooms available for sale in Web City were demanded for the duration of the convention? Then, according to the law of supply, the hoteliers (or at least those hotels with a good revenue management team) would charge the highest reasonable rate possible to maximize revenue.

This is not always the case, however, in either the lodging industry or other industries that utilize revenue management to maximize income. Let's now look at another scenario in Web City. What if the convention is supposed to attract enough attendees to sell 85 percent of the rooms available in Web City for the duration of the convention? This is an example of a situation that requires the skills of a good revenue manager. The individual or team in charge of revenue management should be able to establish a rate that would help maximize the hotel's revenue. If the rate is too low, the hotel might have a 100 percent occupancy rate, but with a less than possible revenue per available room (RevPAR). Similarly, if the rate is too high, the hotel might have the best average daily rate (ADR), but with a less than possible revenue per available room (RevPAR). Hence, the goal of the individual or team in charge of revenue management should be to establish a rate that would help maximize RevPAR.

Revenue Per Available Room (RevPAR)

RevPAR can be defined as the total revenue from room sales divided by the total number of rooms available in the lodging facility. It is the best measure of a lodging facility's ability to maximize total rooms revenue because it is based on the best ADR and occupancy rate possible to maximize room revenue. The formulas for calculating RevPAR are shown below:

Formulas

7.1. RevPAR = Occupancy Percentage × ADR

7.2. $\text{RevPAR} = \dfrac{\text{Total Room Revenue}}{\text{Total \# of Rooms Available}}$

Let's calculate RevPAR using the above Web City scenario. To calculate RevPAR using the Web City scenario you need to know the total room revenue from Web City for the duration of the convention. If the convention attracted enough attendees to sell 85 percent of the rooms available in Web City for the duration of the convention at an ADR of $150, the room revenue is $1,275,000 (8,500 × $150). The total number of rooms available is 10,000 rooms. Eighty-five percent of 10,000 rooms is equal to 8,500 (85% × 10,000) rooms; 8,500 rooms multiplied by the ADR of $150 is equal to $1,275,000.

Using formula 7.1: RevPAR = $127.50 (85% × $150)

Similarly, using formula 7.2: RevPAR = $127.50 ($1,275,000 ÷ 10,000)

The importance of increasing RevPAR cannot be overemphasized. The higher the RevPAR, the higher the profit margin from the rooms' sale. Similarly, the lower the RevPAR, the lower the profit margin from the rooms' sale. This is why RevPAR is the most important measurement of a lodging facility's room revenue and profit. A good property management system (PMS) usually provides RevPAR as part of the daily reports. But it is highly important for managers to know how to calculate RevPAR, occupancy rate, and ADR as a necessary tool for planning revenue maximization. A PMS can assist managers or hoteliers with revenue management decision making, but the system must be programmed in accord with the revenue management philosophy of the individual or team in charge of revenue management.

So far in this chapter, a variety of methods used for establishing initial rack rates have been examined. Hospitality managers, however, must be mindful of the fact that the establishment of rack rates is just the beginning of revenue management. Revenue managers continually make decisions related to potential occupancy rate, special event rate, rate discount management, group rate, negotiated rates, and low/high demand tactics. Each of these variables is an essential element of revenue management that should be considered when making decisions in regard to revenue and profit maximization.

Essentials of Revenue Management

Forecasting Occupancy Rate

Most hotels' property management systems (PMS) are designed with forecasting programs. But hotel management cannot totally depend on the PMS for occupancy forecasts. The PMS may provide the necessary data to guide management in forecasting. In most hotels, the front office manager (FOM) is eventually responsible for the hotel's occupancy forecast. In some economy hotels, the general manager might be in charge of the occupancy forecast; however, for the rest of this chapter the person in charge of forecasting will be referred to as the FOM. It is not uncommon for FOMs to enhance the accuracy of their forecasts by utilizing internal and external reports.

Internal Reports: Internal reports are reports that are generated in a hotel or lodging establishment with the help of PMS or other systems to show the status of the establishment in regard to the occupancy rate, ADR, and RevPAR. FOMs can use internal reports to help enhance the accuracy of the occupancy forecast. Some of the critical reports that should be analyzed include **previous occupancy forecast, reservation activities, occupancy rate, no-shows, early departures, stayovers,** and **cancellations**. These reports can be used collectively to enhance the accuracy of the individual FOM's forecast. For example, an effective FOM will analyze the internal report to see the previous occupancy forecast and reservation activities and compare it with the actual occupancy rate. This analysis will help the FOM determine the differences between the previous year's occupancy forecast, reservation activities, and the actual occupancy rate. The ability of the FOM to analyze the internal report will provide her or him with a better understanding of the implications of no-shows, early departures, stayovers, and cancellations. Having access to the internal report and the ability to analyze it will enable FOMs to enhance the accuracy of their forecasts.

External Reports: In some rare situations (in the case of a new hotel or lodging facility) where an internal report is not available, FOMs can use an external report to help enhance the accuracy of the occupancy forecast. In fact, the use of the external report is not limited to this situation alone. Some effective FOMs utilize the analysis of both the internal and external reports to enhance their occupancy forecasts. FOMs should be aware of the impact of their previous year's rate and other factors on their actual occupancy rate. It is not uncommon for some hotels within the same competitive set to do better than their competitors. FOMs can use external reports to examine their performance (in this case, occupancy rate) as compared with their competitive set. Some sources of external reports include Smith Travel Research (STR) and TravelCLICK. The STR (STAR) report, founded by Randy Smith in 1985, is more comprehensive and commonly used by most users of external reports.

The STAR report is an independent third party collection of summaries of hotels' historical performance data. These data are collected each day from more than 18,000 hotels, and each month from more than 23,000 hotels, which is equivalent to about 2.8 million rooms. These data are provided by reliable sources such as hotels' management companies/staff, hotel chain headquarters, and owners. Some of the data collected from each hotel include the total number of rooms available, number of rooms sold, and total room revenue. This information is then used to compute different statistical variables that are useful for the daily operations of hotels and lodging facilities such as each property's:

- Occupancy rate
- RevPar
- ADR
- Competitive set occupancy rate
- Competitive set RevPar
- Competitive set ADR
- Occupancy index
- RevPar index
- ADR index

A major advantage of external reports is that they can be used to evaluate the previous year's decisions. Hence, external report products such as the occupancy index can be used by management to evaluate the effectiveness of the property's occupancy decisions.

Occupancy Index

Occupancy index is a good tool for measuring a property's occupancy performance. The occupancy index is computed by dividing the occupancy rate of the subject property by the occupancy rate of its competitive set. The occupancy index could be used by management to see how its occupancy rate and the factors (e.g., rate) that led to that occupancy rate compares with other properties within the same competitive set.

Formulas

7.3. Occupancy Index of Hotel "A" $= \dfrac{\text{Occupancy Rate of Hotel "A"}}{\text{Occupancy Rate of Competitive Set Hotels}}$

To understand how the occupancy index could help FOMs enhance occupancy rates and revenue, consider the following data for a hotel and its competitive set hotels with one hundred rooms each.

The data show that Paradise Hotel achieved an occupancy index of 135.71% (95% ÷ 70%), while its competitive set achieved an occupancy index of 73.68 (70% ÷ 95%). The result of this occupancy index indicates that Paradise Hotel sold more rooms compared with its competitive set hotels. But when you examine the revenue between Paradise Hotel and its competitive set hotels, the competitive set hotels generated more revenue than Paradise Hotel. Paradise Hotel generated $4,750 ($47.50 × 100 rooms) for that period; whereas, its competitive set hotels generated $6,930 ($69.30 × 100 rooms) during the same period. Effective management should be mindful of this scenario when forecasting occupancy and determining rate for the next fiscal year. Although Paradise Hotel had a better occupancy index than its competitive set hotels, it wasn't enough to help management maximize the property's revenue.

Bearing the above in mind, the occupancy index could be a benchmark for measuring the effectiveness of management's occupancy forecast decisions, if the hotel's rates are not significantly different from the rates of its competitive set hotels. Effective management or a FOM should use the occupancy index to adjust the hotel's occupancy forecast from one year to another. The point is that when determining occupancy forecast, a FOM should consider the hotel's room rate and the potential rates of its competitive set hotels. When using the occupancy index to enhance the occupancy forecast in an area that maintains a similar economic condition from one fiscal year to the next, FOMs should consider the following:

1. If the occupancy index is a lot less than 100 percent but the ADR is a lot more than the ADR of the competitive set hotels, management should do one of the following:
   - Decrease rack rates on rooms as necessary to be a little more than the rack rates of the competitive set hotels' previous year rates, and keep the occupancy forecast for the next fiscal year more than the previous year's actual occupancy rate.
   - Decrease rack rates on rooms as necessary to be equivalent to the rack rates of the competitive set hotels' previous year rates, and keep the occupancy forecast for the next fiscal year more than the previous year's actual occupancy rate.

Exhibit 7.2: Comparison of Occupancy Index

Hotels	Occupancy Rate	ADR	RevPAR	Occupancy Index
Paradise Hotel	95%	$50.00	$47.50	135.71
Competitive Set Hotels	70%	$99.00	$69.30	73.68

2. If the occupancy index is more than 100 percent but the ADR is much less than the ADR of the competitive set hotels, management should do one of the following:
   - Increase rack rates (or eliminate discounts) on rooms as necessary to be a little less than the rack rates of the competitive set hotels' previous year rates, and keep the occupancy forecast for the next fiscal year the same as the previous year's actual occupancy rate.
   - Increase rack rates (or eliminate discounts) on rooms as necessary to be the equivalent to the rack rates of the competitive set hotels' previous year rates, and keep the occupancy forecast for the next fiscal year a little less than the previous year's actual occupancy rate.
3. If the occupancy index is more than 100 percent but the ADR is equivalent to the ADR of the competitive set hotels, management should do following:
   - Increase rack rates (or eliminate discounts) on rooms as necessary to be more than the rack rates of the previous year, and keep the occupancy forecast for the next fiscal year a little less than the previous year's actual occupancy rate.
4. If the occupancy index and ADR are both equivalent to those of the competitive set hotels, management should do following:
   - Increase rack rates (or eliminate discounts) on rooms as necessary to be more than the rack rates of the previous year, and keep the occupancy forecast for the next fiscal year equivalent to the previous year's actual occupancy rate.

Impact of the Economy and Special Event(s): FOMs should to be aware of the implications of the local and regional economy and special events on their occupancy percentage. If the economy is great and corporations, government, and associations are having more meetings and events, the ability to demand and pay more for rooms usually increases. Hence, FOMs should pay careful attention to economic trends and their impact on local meetings and events. Usually, more meetings and events lead to an increased demand for rooms. The larger the group coming to a community, the better the chance of eliminating discounts or increasing the rack rates while achieving a high occupancy percentage. Hence, FOMs should be able to consider this phenomenon to enhance their facilities' occupancy forecasts and revenue.

MLOS and CTA: If the demand for rooms is very high on a particular day (e.g., Monday) of the week, but low on the day before that day (Sunday) and the day after that day (Tuesday), in order for the revenue manager to maximize RevPAR for the week he or she should work with the FOM to increase occupancy by identifying Monday as the **minimum length of stay (MLOS)** day. That is, those who want to stay in the hotel on Monday will have to stay for a minimum of two nights. Bearing the above in mind, those requesting Monday night will have to include Sunday night or Tuesday or more nights to be able to secure rooms in this situation.

Close to arrival (CTA) is another tactic that could be used to increase occupancy instead of MLOS. CTA refers to a hotel's ability to decline room reservations for guests desiring to arrive on a busy day for just one night, in an attempt to encourage guests to make reservations for two nights or more. Using the previous MLOS example, if a guest desires to arrive on a busy Monday, CTA will require the guest to arrive on Sunday by reserving Sunday and Monday or more rooms. By requiring guests to arrive on Sunday, the FOM will be enhancing total weekend occupancy by increasing Sunday night occupancy. FOMs and revenue managers, however, should be careful when implementing MLOS and CTA because they could negatively affect the occupancy rate. To prevent MLOS and CTA from negatively affecting the occupancy rate, FOMs should be very skillful about the following:

- Percentage of rooms that must be reserved via MLOS or CTA
- Dates where MLOS or CTA might be used
- Being very careful not to upset loyal customers because of the application of MLOS or CTA

Sometimes it is better for the sake of revenue maximization if the FOM avoids the use of CTA because CTA tactics might deny a room reservation to a guest who may have wished to stay for many nights. For example, a guest who wishes to arrive on Monday and stay for two weeks would be denied a reservation if the CTA tactic is used. For the above reasons, FOMs should be skillful about when to use MLOS and CTA to enhance the occupancy rate or forecast.

Rate and Discount Management

So far within the essentials of revenue management, you have learned about the implications of the following factors: local and regional economy, special events, and appropriate occupancy forecast for revenue maximization purposes. None of the above factors, however, will be effective without the appropriate rate and discount management. Earlier in this chapter you also learned about rack rate and different pricing strategies. Knowing how to establish the rack rate is good, but knowing when to increase the rack rate and curtail discounts are even better for revenue management purposes. Just as FOMs utilize internal and external reports to enhance the accuracy of their facility's occupancy forecast, similarly, revenue managers should utilize internal and external reports to enhance the accuracy of rate and discount management.

ADR Index

When examining the internal report, revenue managers should explore how negotiated rates for large groups and room discounts affected the ADRs of previous years. In addition, the external report will be very useful for examining the ADR index and RevPAR index. If a hotel's ADR is close to the ADR of its competitive set, the ADR index will be close to 100 percent the closer the ADR index to 100 percent is, the more the ADR index will be a good measure of the hotel's effectiveness in room rate and discount management.

Formulas

7.4. ADR Index of Hotel "A" $= \dfrac{\text{ADR of Hotel "A"}}{\text{ADR of Competitive Set Hotels}}$

7.5. RevPAR Index of Hotel "A" $= \dfrac{\text{RevPAR of Hotel "A"}}{\text{RevPAR of Competitive Set Hotels}}$

Exhibit 7.3: Comparison of ADR and RevPAR Indexes

Hotels	Occupancy Rate	ADR	ADR Index	RevPAR	RevPAR Index
Paradise Hotel	95%	$50.00	50.51	$47.50	68.54
Competitive Set Hotels	70%	$99.00	198.00	$69.30	145.89

To understand how the examination of the previous years' ADR index could help revenue managers enhance room rate and discount management, consider the following data for a hotel and its competitive set hotels with one hundred rooms each.

The data show that Paradise Hotel achieved an ADR index of 50.51 ($50 ÷ $99), while its competitive set achieved an ADR index of 198.00 ($99 ÷ $50). Obviously, Paradise Hotel's ADR is very low compared with its competitive set hotels' ADR. As a result, even though Paradise Hotel sold more rooms than its competitive set hotels, the RevPAR of its competitive set hotels are significantly higher than the RevPAR of Paradise Hotel. Similarly, Paradise Hotel achieved a lower RevPAR index of 68.54 ($47.50 ÷ $69.30) than its competitive set RevPAR index of 145.89 ($69.30 ÷ $47.50). For this reason, Paradise Hotel generated less revenue than its competitive set hotels. Paradise Hotel generated $4,750 ($47.50 × 100 rooms) for that period; whereas it's competitive set hotels generated $6,930 ($69.30 × 100 rooms) during the same period. Based on the above examples, to be able to make the changes needed to maximize the hotel's revenue, an effective revenue manager should be concerned about why his or her ADR index and/or RevPAR index is less than their competitive sets. It is common knowledge among many hoteliers that hotels' occupancy rates are associated with their sales and marketing abilities. Similarly, many hoteliers relate ADR to guests' expectations of a hotel's quality. If a hotel's quality meets or exceeds guests' expectations in relation to room rates paid, they are likely to return. It is very critical for revenue managers to establish room rates that will satisfy or exceed their guests' expectations of quality. When using the ADR index to enhance the room rates and discount management, management should consider the following:

1. If the ADR index is a lot less than 100 percent but the occupancy index is above 100 percent, management should do one of the following depending on the quality of the hotel and its sales and marketing efforts:

- Increase rack rates on rooms as necessary to be about the same as the rack rates of the competitive set hotels' previous year rack rates, curtail discounts during busy periods, and keep the occupancy forecast for the next fiscal year close to the competitive set hotels' previous year actual occupancy rates.
- Increase rack rates on rooms as necessary to be a little more than the rack rate of the competitive set hotels' previous year rack rates, curtail discounts during busy periods, and keep the occupancy forecast for the next fiscal year close to the competitive set hotels' previous year actual occupancy rates.

2. If the ADR index is more than 100 percent but the occupancy index is a lot less than 100 percent, management should do one of the following:
   - Decrease rack rates on rooms as necessary to be as close to the competitive set hotels' previous year rack rates, consider offering discounts (especially during slow periods), and keep the occupancy forecast for the next fiscal year very close to the competitive set hotels' previous year actual occupancy rates.
   - Decrease rack rates on rooms as necessary but keep it a little more than the rack rates of the competitive set hotels' previous year rack rates, consider offering discounts (especially during slow periods), and keep the occupancy forecast for the next fiscal year very close to the competitive set hotels' previous year actual occupancy rates.

3. If the ADR index is more than 100 percent but the occupancy index is equivalent to the competitive set hotels' occupancy index, management should do one of the following:
   - Increase rack rates on rooms as necessary (depending on demand and supply) to a level more than the rack rates of the previous year, and keep the occupancy forecast for the next fiscal year the same as the previous year's actual occupancy rate.
   - Keep rack rates on rooms the same but curtail discounts on rooms as much as possible, and keep the occupancy forecast for the next fiscal year the same as the previous year's actual occupancy rate.

4. If the ADR index is equivalent to the competitive set hotels' ADR index but the occupancy index is above 100 percent, management should do one of the following:
   - Increase rack rates on rooms as necessary to be a little above the rack rates of the previous year's rack rates, curtail discounts during busy periods, and keep the occupancy forecast for the next fiscal year very close to the previous year's actual occupancy rate.
   - Keep rack rates on rooms the same but curtail discounts on rooms as much as possible, and keep the occupancy forecast for the next fiscal year very close to the previous year's actual occupancy rate.

RevPAR Index

RevPAR index is the best measurement of a lodging facility's room revenue management. A RevPAR index usually indicates the impact of the combination of the ADR and occupancy index. A RevPAR index above 100 percent implies that a hotel is doing better than its competitive set hotels in terms of revenue management. When a hotel's RevPAR index is around 100 percent, it generally implies that the hotel's occupancy rate and ADR complements each other very well. In other words, the FOM's occupancy forecast and the revenue manager's ADR is just right. But if a hotel's RevPAR index is less than 100 percent, it generally that implies that the hotel's occupancy rate and/or ADR is lower than the competitors. In other words, the FOM's occupancy forecast and the revenue manager's ADR are ineffective. When using the RevPAR index for revenue management, management should consider the following:

1. If the RevPAR index is a lot less than 100 percent but the occupancy index is around 100 percent, management should do one of the following depending on the quality of the hotel and its sales and marketing efforts:
   - Increase rack rates on rooms as necessary to be about the same as the rack rates of the competitive set hotels, increase discounts if the ADR index is above 100 percent, and keep the occupancy forecast for the next fiscal year very close to the competitive set hotels' previous year actual occupancy rates.
   - Increase rack rates on rooms as necessary to be a little more than the rack rate of the competitive set hotels' previous year rack rates, curtail discounts if the ADR index is well below 100 percent, and keep the occupancy forecast for the next fiscal year very close to the competitive set hotels' previous year actual occupancy rates.
2. If the RevPAR index and occupancy index is well below 100 percent, management should do one of the following:
   - If ADR index is above 100 percent, decrease rack rates on rooms as necessary to be as close to the competitive set hotels' previous year rack rates, consider increasing discounts, and keep the occupancy forecast for the next fiscal year very close to the competitive set hotels' previous year actual occupancy rates.
   - Increase rack rates on rooms and curtail discounts if the ADR index is well below 100 percent, and keep the occupancy forecast for the next fiscal year very close to the competitive set hotels' previous year actual occupancy rates.

It is very crucial for revenue managers to be mindful that hotels' revenue maximization requires the effort of all hotel employees. In addition to the revenue manager's decision making, a host of other factors could negatively affect the hotel's RevPAR index, bringing it lower than that of its competitive set hotels. These factors include:

1. Poor sales and marketing effort
2. Inadequate room cleanliness
3. Unappealing brand or franchise
4. Poor property access and/or exterior signage
5. Poor decorations and furnishings
6. Poor facility maintenance
7. Inadequate distribution channels
8. Lack of adequate employees' support

The first seven factors are usual operational concerns that most managements should be aware of and budget for. On the other hand, the eighth factor requires the efforts of a dedicated revenue manager to mobilize the employees, secure their support, and work hard to continuously maintain the revenue management philosophy of the organization. A **revenue management**

meeting is a good approach to securing employees' support. A revenue management meeting can be described as a meeting of an organization's department heads with the purpose of enhancing the organization's revenue management philosophy and garnering the support of the concerned departments and employees.

Revenue Management Meeting

When planning a revenue management meeting, the revenue manager should consider the following:

- Attendees: All the organization's department heads (e.g., revenue manager-lead the meeting, general manager, controller, director of sales and marketing, director of reservation/front office manager, food and beverage director/restaurant managers, chief engineer/maintenance, human resources manager, executive housekeepers, etc.).
- Purpose: Focus on the purpose of the meeting, identify and suggest revenue opportunities for the facility, discuss the results of your internal and external analysis of past performance (ADR, RevPAR, occupancy rate, and the indexes).
- Discuss the current sales and marketing efforts (work with the director of sales and marketing).
- Discuss the slow and busy periods in the facility.
- Share the proposed forecast for the period at the meeting (work with the front office manager).
- Discuss the suggested sales and marketing efforts (work with the director of sales and marketing).
- Share your proposed revenue maximization plan and the basis of your suggestions, including suggested rates per room during busy and slow periods.
- Discuss the importance of each department and employees' support for the revenue management plan to work. Some form of employee motivation could be very helpful to gain the support of employees.
- Solicit suggestions from the meeting and ensure the support of department heads.

Spreadsheet-Modeling Approach for Revenue Management

EXAMPLE 7.1

Scenario: As the front office manager (FOM) of a 350-room Paradise luxury resort, you have been asked to prepare a revenue maximization projection of room sales for the next fiscal year. Your first step is to reflect on the following factors:

- Internal reports
- External reports
- Local, regional, and national economic factors
- Local competitions
- Sales and marketing efforts, etc.

After rational and careful reflection of the above factors and current trends in the industry, you have a reason to believe that the local economy will grow by 4 percent. The country's inflation is running at 2 percent. You also noticed that last year remodeling schedule affected room revenue. To enhance the revenue for the next fiscal year you decide to change some monthly occupancy forecasts but keep some of the more justifiable monthly occupancy rates from last year (March, April, August, September, and October) the same while increasing last year's monthly rates by 2 percent to offset inflation. The monthly actual occupancy rate and ADR for the previous year are shown in Exhibit 7.4.

Exhibit 7.4: Previous Occupancy Rate and ADR

	Occupancy Rate (%)	ADR ($)	Rationale for Occupancy Rate and ADR
January	60	195	
February	100	210	PCMA/other conferences booked
March	82	210	NCAA sports
April	80	210	NCAA sports
May	78	200	Multiple graduations
June	50	200	Lost group reservation in both months due to inadequate facility maintenance
July	50	200	
August	96	210	Annual festival
September	96	210	Corporate conference booked
October	82	210	NCAA sports
November	46	175	Remodeling of guest rooms
December	40	175	Remodeling continues

As the FOM, your projected occupancy rate for each month in the next fiscal year, designed to enhance revenue, is shown in Exhibit 7.5.

Exhibit 7.5: The Occupancy Rate Projection for the Next Fiscal Year

	Occupancy Rate (%) Projected	Rationale for Occupancy Rate Projected
January	66	
February	90	Corporate convention booked
March	82	NCAA sports
April	80	NCAA sports
May	80	Multiple graduations
June	80	Special events/rooms are
July	80	remodeled
August	96	Annual festival

September	96	Corporate conference booked	
October	82	NCAA sports	
November	72	Rooms remodeled/events	
December	76	Multiple graduations	

Questions:

1. What is the previous year's number of rooms sold?
2. What is the previous year's revenue?
3. What is the next fiscal year's projected number of rooms to be sold?
4. What is the next fiscal year's projected revenue?
5. What is the difference between the previous year's and the next fiscal year's revenue?
6. What is the previous year's annual occupancy rate?
7. What is the previous year's ADR?
8. What is the previous year's RevPAR?
9. What is the next fiscal year's annual occupancy rate?
10. What is the next fiscal year's ADR?
11. What is the next fiscal year's RevPAR?
12. Do you agree with the rationale for the occupancy rate projected for the next fiscal year? If you were to attempt anything different, what would you do?

ANSWER: To solve this question, you need to be familiar with the following formulas as initially outlined in Formulas 1.5–1.9, remember the spreadsheet design guiding principles in Chapter 1 (as also listed in Exhibit 4.3), and follow the step-by-step, hands-on approach to Example 7.1 as outlined below. Start by computing the previous year's revenue schedule, and then using the same approach compute the next fiscal year's revenue schedule and answer the scenario's questions.

Formulas

7.6. Revenue = Average Daily Rate (ADR) × Volume (# of rooms sold)

7.7. $ADR = \dfrac{\text{Total Room Revenue}}{\text{Total \# of Rooms Sold}}$

7.8. Total Rooms Sold = Occupancy Rate × Total # of Rooms Available

7.9. $\text{Occupancy Rate} = \dfrac{\text{Total Rooms Sold}}{\text{Total \# of Rooms Available}}$

STEP-BY-STEP, HANDS-ON APPROACH TO EXAMPLE 7.1

1. In your Excel spreadsheet, start with the headings by inserting *# of Rooms in Hotel =* and *350* in cells A2 and B2, respectively.
2. Following the first set of headings, insert *Months, Occupancy Rate, ADR ($), # of Days/Month, # of Rooms Sold/Day, # of Rooms Sold/Month,* and *Previous Year's Revenue ($)* in cells A3 and B4, C3 and C4, D3 and D4, E3 and E4, F3 and F4, and G3 and G4, respectively.
3. Insert each month in a year below the *Months* heading in cells A5–A16.
4. Similarly, inserts the given occupancy rate (see Exhibit 7.4) corresponding to each month below the *Occupancy Rate* heading in cells B5–B16.
5. Also inserts the given ADR (see Exhibit 7.4) corresponding to each month below the *ADR ($)* heading in cells C5–C16.
6. Also insert the number of days per each month in the *# of Days/Month* heading in cells D5–D16.

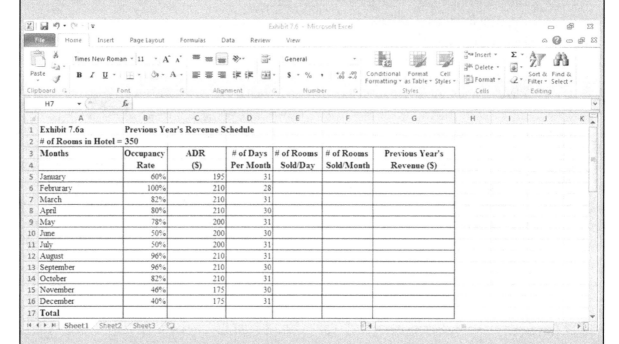

7. Compute the number of rooms sold per day for each month below the *# of Rooms Sold/Day* heading in cells E5–E16. You will need Formula 7.5:

$$\text{Occupancy Rate} = \frac{\text{Total Rooms Sold}}{\text{Total \# of Rooms Available}}$$

$$\left[\text{Total Rooms Sold/Day}\right] = \left[\text{Occupancy Rate}\right] \times \left[\begin{array}{l}\text{Total \# of Rooms} \\ \text{Available}\end{array}\right]$$

8. *To compute the number of rooms sold per day in January,* select the cell in which you want to place the formula (i.e., E5).

9. Type an equal sign (=) to start the formula. Click the first cell you want to place in the formula (i.e., B2). When you click the cell, a border surrounds the cell indicating the cell you are working with and its name appears on the formula bar. Next, type the asterisk (*) key to the formula bar to form [=B2*]. Click the second cell you want to place in the formula (i.e., B5) to form [=B2*B5], then press the enter key. Excel calculates the result and displays it in the cell as **210**.

10. *To compute the number of rooms sold per day for the rest of the months*, double click cell E5 (210) to modify the formula.

11. Add a dollar sign ($) in front of letter "B" and number "2" to form [=$B$2*B5] in order to keep cell B2 constant for each month's computation.

12. Then copy the cell E5 (210) and paste it into cells E6–E16 for the automatic computation of the rest of the months (i.e., February = E6 = 350, March = E7 = 287, April = E8 = 280 … December = E16 = 140).

13. After computing the number of rooms sold per day as computed above, it is time to compute the number of rooms sold per month.

14. Compute the number of rooms sold per month below the *# of Rooms Sold/Month* heading in cells F5–F16.

15. *To compute the number of rooms sold per January*, select the cell in which you want to place the formula (i.e., F5).

16. Type an equal sign (=) to start the formula. Click the first cell you want to place in the formula (i.e., E5). When you click the cell, a border surrounds the cell indicating the cell you are working with and its name appears on the formula bar. Next, type the asterisk (*) key to the formula bar to form [=E5*]. Click the second cell you want to place in the formula (i.e., D5) to form [=E5*D5], then press the enter key. Excel calculates the result and displays it in the cell as **6510**.

17. *To compute the number of rooms sold per month for the rest of the months*, just copy cell F5 (6510) and paste in each of the other cells below the *# of Rooms Sold/Month* heading.

18. If cell F5 (6510) is copied and pasted correctly into cells F6–F16 for the automatic computation of the rest of the months, you should have the following: February = F6 = 9800, March = F7 = 8897, April = F8 = 8400 … December = F16 = 4340.

19. Now you can compute the revenue per each month below the *Previous Year's Revenue ($)* heading in cells G5–G16.

20. You will need Formula 7.1:

> Revenue = (ADR) × (# of Rooms Sold)
> Revenue/Month = (ADR) × (# of Rooms Sold/Month)

21. *To compute the revenue per month for January* of the previous year's revenue, select the cell in which you want to place the formula (i.e., G5).

22. Type an equal sign (=) to start the formula. Click the first cell you want to place in the formula (i.e., C5). When you click the cell, a border surrounds the cell indicating the cell you are working with and its name appears on the formula bar. Next, type the asterisk (*) key to the formula bar to form [=C5*]. Click the second cell you want to place in the formula (i.e., F5) to form [=C5*F5], then press the enter key. Excel calculates the result and displays it in the cell as **$1,269,450**.

23. *To compute the revenue per month for the rest of the months*, just copy cell G5 ($1,269,450) and paste in each of the other cells below the *Previous Year's Revenue ($)* heading.

24. If cell G5 ($1,269,450) is copied and pasted correctly into cells G6–G16 for the automatic computation of the rest of the months' revenue, you should have the following: February = G6 = $2,058,000; March = G7 = $1,868,370; April = G8 = $1,764,000 . . . December = G16 = $759,500.

25. Now that each month's variables are computed, you can now *calculate the total number of rooms sold and the total revenue for the previous year*.

> Total # of Rooms Sold = The Sum of All the # of Rooms Sold/Month
> Total Previous Year's Revenue = The Sum of All the Monthly Revenue

26. Start by inserting "Total" in cell A17. Then select the cell in which you want to place the total number of rooms sold for the previous year (i.e., F17).

27. Type an equal sign (=) to start the formula. Since you are adding more than two variables, you could use the sum function to make it faster. Hence, type in SUM after the equal sign (=) followed with an open parenthesis to form [=SUM( ]. Select the cells you want to sum up in the formula (i.e., F5:F16). When you select the cells, a border surrounds the cells indicating the cell you are summing up, which will appear on the formula bar. Next, insert the close parenthesis to form [=SUM(F5:F16)], then press the enter key. Excel calculates the result and displays it in the cell as **91,308**.

28. Similarly, select the cell in which you want to place the total previous year's revenue formula (i.e., G17).

29. Type an equal sign (=) to start the formula. Since you are adding more than two variables, you could use the sum function to make it faster. Hence, type in SUM after the equal sign (=) followed with an open parenthesis to form [=SUM( ]. Select the cells you want to sum up in the formula (i.e., G5:G16). When you select the cells, a border surrounds the cells indicating the cell you are summing up, which will appear on the formula bar. Next, insert the close parenthesis to form [=SUM(G5:G16)], then press the enter key. Excel calculates the result and displays it in the cell as **$18,564,700**.

30. Now that you are done computing the total previous year's revenue, you are ready *to compute the next fiscal year's revenue*.

31. In your Excel spreadsheet following Exhibit 7.6a, start with the headings by inserting *Months, Occupancy Rate, 2% Increase ADR ($), # of Days/Month, P# of Rooms Sold/Day, P# of Rooms Sold/Month*, and *P Next Fiscal Year's Revenue ($)* in cells A20, B20 and B21, C20 and C21, D20 and D21, E20 and E21, F20 and F21, and G20 and G21, respectively.

32. Insert each month in a year below the *Months* heading in cells A22–A33.

33. Similarly, inserts the given occupancy rate (see Exhibit 7.4) corresponding to each month below the *Occupancy Rate* heading in cells B22–B33.

34. Then compute the 2 percent increase in ADR corresponding to each month below the *2% Increase ADR ($)* heading in cells C22–C33. Start by selecting the cell in which you want to place January's 2 percent increase in the ADR formula (i.e., C22).

35. Type an equal sign (=) to start the formula. Type the amount you want to increase by 2 percent in the formula (i.e., 195). Next, type the plus (+) key to form [=195+].

36. Next, insert the open parenthesis to form [=195+(], then type 2% to form [=195+(2%].

37. Then insert the asterisk (*) key to the formula bar to form [=195+(2%*)], then type the amount you want to increase by 2 percent to form [=195+(2%*195)]. Insert the close parenthesis to form [=195+(2%*195)], then press the enter key. Excel calculates the result and displays it in the cell as **$198.90**.

38. Repeat steps 35–37 for the remaining months (i.e., February–December), but replacing 195 with the appropriate amount (see Exhibit 7.4 ADR) for each month.

39. Then insert the number of days per each month in the # *of Days/Month* heading in cells D22–D33.

40. Compute the projected number of rooms sold per day for each month below the *P# of Rooms Sold/Day* heading in cells E22–E33. You will need Formula 7.5 as displayed in Step 7 above.

41. *To compute the projected number of rooms sold per day in January*, select the cell in which you want to place the formula (i.e., E22).

42. Type an equal sign (=) to start the formula. Click the first cell you want to place in the formula (i.e., B2). When you click the cell, a border surrounds the cell indicating the cell you are working with and its name appears on the formula bar. Next, type the asterisk (*) key to the formula bar to form [=B2*]. Click the second cell you want to place in the formula (i.e., B22) to form [=B2*B22], then press the enter key. Excel calculates the result and displays it in the cell as **231**.

43. *To compute the number of rooms sold per day for the rest of the months*, double click cell E22 (231) to modify the formula.

44. Add a dollar sign ($) in front of letter "B" and number "2" to form [=$B$2*B22] in order to keep cell B2 constant for each month's computation.

45. Then copy the cell E22 (231) and paste it into cells E23–E33 for the automatic computation of the rest of the months (i.e., February = E23 = 315, March = E24 = 287, April = E25 = 280 . . . December = E33 = 266).

46. After computing the projected number of rooms sold per day as computed above, it's time to compute the projected number of rooms sold per month.

47. Compute the projected number of rooms sold per month below the *P# of Rooms Sold/Month* heading in cells F22–F33.

48. *To compute the projected number of rooms sold per January*, select the cell in which you want to place the formula (i.e., F22).

49. Type an equal sign (=) to start the formula. Click the first cell you want to place in the formula (i.e., E22). When you click the cell, a border surrounds the cell indicating the cell you are working with and its name appears on the formula bar. Next, type the asterisk (*) key to the formula bar to form [=E22*]. Click the second cell you want to place in the formula (i.e., D22) to form [=E22*D22], then press the enter key. Excel calculates the result and displays it in the cell as **7161**.

50. *To compute the projected number of rooms sold per month for the rest of the months*, just copy cell F22 (7161) and paste in each of the other cells below the *P# of Rooms Sold/Month* heading.

51. If cell F22 (7161) is copied and pasted correctly into cells F23–F33 for the automatic computation of the rest of the months, you should have the following: February = F23 = 8820, March = F24 = 8897, April = F25 = 8400 . . . December = F33 = 8246.

52. Now you can compute the projected revenue per each month below the *P Next Year's Revenue ($)* heading in cells G22–G33.

53. You will need Formula 7.1:

> Revenue = (ADR) × (# of Rooms Sold)
>
> Revenue/Month = (ADR) × (# of Rooms Sold/Month)

54. *To compute the projected revenue per month for January* of the projected next year's revenue, select the cell in which you want to place the formula (i.e., G22).

55. Type an equal sign (=) to start the formula. Click the first cell you want to place in the formula (i.e., C22). When you click the cell, a border surrounds the cell indicating the cell you are working with and its name appears on the formula bar. Next, type the asterisk (*) key to the formula bar to form [=C22*]. Click the second cell you want to place in the formula (i.e., F22) to form [=C22*F22], then press the enter key. Excel calculates the result and displays it in the cell as **$1,424,322.90**.

56. *To compute the projected revenue per month for the rest of the months,* just copy cell G22 ($1,424,322.90) and paste in each of the other cells below the "*P Next Year's Revenue ($)*" heading.

57. If cell G22 ($1,424,322.90) is copied and pasted correctly into cells G23–G33 for the automatic computation of the rest of the months' revenue, you should have the following: February = G23 = $1,889,244.00; March = G24 = $1,905,737.40; April = G25 = $1,799,280.00 . . . December = G33 = $1,471,911.

58. Now that each month's variables are computed, you can now *calculate the total projected number of rooms sold and the total projected revenue for the next fiscal year.*

> Total # of Rooms Sold = The Sum of All the # of Rooms Sold/Month
>
> Total Next Fiscal Year's Revenue = The Sum of All the Monthly Revenue

59. Start by inserting "Total" in cell A34. Then select the cell in which you want to place the projected total number of rooms sold for the next fiscal year (i.e., F34).

60. Type an equal sign (=) to start the formula. Since you are adding more than two variables, you could use the sum function to make it faster. Hence, type in SUM after the equal sign (=) followed with an open parenthesis to form [=SUM( ]. Select the cells you want to sum up in the formula (i.e., F22:F33). When you select the cells, a border surrounds the cells indicating the cell you are summing up, which will appear on the formula bar. Next, insert the close parenthesis to form [=SUM(F22:F33)], then press the enter key. Excel calculates the result and displays it in the cell as **104,237**.

61. Similarly, select the cell in which you want to place the total projected next fiscal year's revenue formula (i.e., G34).

62. Type an equal sign (=) to start the formula. Since you are adding more than two variables, you could use the sum function to make it faster. Hence, type in SUM after the equal sign (=) followed with an open parenthesis to form [=SUM( ]. Select the cells you want to sum up in the formula (i.e., G22:G33). When you select the cells, a border surrounds the cells indicating the cell you are summing up, which will appear on the formula bar. Next, insert the close parenthesis to form [=SUM(G22:G33)], then press the enter key. Excel calculates the result and displays it in the cell as **$21,390,975.90**.

By following the above instructions you should be done preparing the previous year's revenue and the projected next fiscal year's revenue. If you make any mistakes in typing any of numbers, do not panic. Just make the necessary changes and all the calculations will be automatically corrected. The result of the spreadsheet-modeling approach to Example 7.1 is displayed in Exhibit 7.6. Now that the spreadsheet modeling is done, you can easily answer the twelve questions relating to this example.

Question 1: What is the previous year's number of rooms sold?
    Answer: = F17 = **91,308**

Question 2: What is the previous year's revenue?
    Answer: = G17 = **$18,564,700**

Question 3: What is the next fiscal year's projected number of rooms to be sold?
    Answer: = F34 = **104,237**

Question 4: What is the next fiscal year's projected revenue?
    Answer: = G34 = **$21,390,975.90**

Question 5: What is the difference between the previous year's and the next fiscal year's revenue?
    Answer: = G34 − G17
            = $21,390,975.90 − $18,564,700
            = **$2,826,275.90**

Exhibit 7.6: Spreadsheet-Modeling Approach to Example 7.1

Exhibit 7.6a   Previous Year's Revenue Schedule
# of Rooms in Hotel = 350

Months	Occupancy Rate	ADR ($)	# of Days Per Month	# of Rooms Sold/Day	# of Rooms Sold/Month	Previous Year's Revenue ($)
January	60%	195	31	210	6510	$1,269,450.00
February	100%	210	28	350	9800	$2,058,000.00
March	82%	210	31	287	8897	$1,868,370.00
April	80%	210	30	280	8400	$1,764,000.00
May	78%	200	31	273	8463	$1,692,600.00
June	50%	200	30	175	5250	$1,050,000.00
July	50%	200	31	175	5425	$1,085,000.00
August	96%	210	31	336	10416	$2,187,360.00
September	96%	210	30	336	10080	$2,116,800.00
October	82%	210	31	287	8897	$1,868,370.00
November	46%	175	30	161	4830	$845,250.00
December	40%	175	31	140	4340	$759,500.00
Total					91,308	$18,564,700.00

Exhibit 7.6b   Next Fiscal Year Revenue Schedule

Months	Occupancy Rate	2% Increased ADR ($)	# of Days Per Month	P # of Rooms Sold/Day	P # of Rooms Sold/Month	P Next Fiscal Year's Revenue ($)
January	66%	198.90	31	231	7161	$1,424,322.90
February	90%	214.20	28	315	8820	$1,889,244.00
March	82%	214.20	31	287	8897	$1,905,737.40
April	80%	214.20	30	280	8400	$1,799,280.00
May	80%	204.00	31	280	8680	$1,770,720.00
June	80%	204.00	30	280	8400	$1,713,600.00
July	80%	204.00	31	280	8680	$1,770,720.00
August	96%	214.20	31	336	10416	$2,231,107.20
September	96%	214.20	30	336	10080	$2,159,136.00
October	82%	214.20	31	287	8897	$1,905,737.40
November	72%	178.50	30	252	7560	$1,349,460.00
December	76%	178.50	31	266	8246	$1,471,911.00
Total					104,237	$21,390,975.90

Note: P = Projected

Question 6: What is the previous year's annual occupancy rate?

Answer: $= F17/(B2 * 365)$

$= 91,308/(350 * 365)$

$= 91,308/127,750$

$= 0.7147$

$= \underline{\textbf{71.47\%}}$

Question 7: What is the previous year's ADR?

Answer: $= G17/F17$

$= \$18,564,700/91,308$

$= \underline{\textbf{\$203.32}}$

Question 8: What is the previous year's RevPAR?

    Answer: = G17/(B2*365)

            = $18,564,700/(350*365)

            = $18,564,700/127,750

            = $145.32

Question 9: What is the next fiscal year's annual occupancy rate?

    Answer: = F34/(B2*365)

            = 104,237/(350*365)

            = 104,237/127,750

            = 0.8159

            = 81.59%

Question 10: What is the next fiscal year's ADR?

    Answer: = G34/F34

            = $21,390,975.90/104,237

            = $205.21

Question 11: What is the next fiscal year's RevPAR?

    Answer: = G34/(B2*365)

            = $21,390,975.90/(350*365)

            = $21,390,975.90/127,750

            = $167.44

Question 12: Do you agree with the rationale for the occupancy rate projected for the next fiscal year? If you were to attempt anything different, what would you do?

Answer: The response to this question will vary. But students should be aware that the rationale for the projected occupancy rate for the next fiscal year is credible. For example, the month of February might experience a decrease in occupancy rate due to the fact that PCMA, which is a large association coupled with other conferences that were booked in the previous year, will be replaced by a corporate convention. Hence, the February occupancy rate that was 100 percent in the previous year could be easily reduced to 90 percent in the next fiscal year—unless the hotel is able to secure more group reservations. In addition, June and July both lost group reservations due to inadequate facility maintenance in the previous year. Since the facility was remodeled for the next fiscal year coupled with the special events, which will bring in more groups during those months, it is very realistic for those months' occupancy rates to increase from 50 percent to 80 percent each. Similarly, November and December would also show increases in the occupancy rate after the facility maintenance and guest room renovations.

ACCOUNTING AND FINANCIAL TERMINOLOGY

ADR *stands for average daily rate, which can be computed by dividing rooms' revenue by the number of rooms sold.*

Check around competitive pricing *is a pricing strategy in which a hotel can use the website to select a competitive set of hotel rates to be monitored, check out the real-time room rates offered by these hotels, and determine a competitive rate to charge in relation to the hotel's competitive set.*

Demand (occupancy) *refers to the number of rooms sold.*

External reports *are external performance data on thousands of hotels that can be used to make rate or pricing-related decisions.*

Fiscal year *is the twelve-month accounting period used by business organizations.*

Follow the leader pricing *is a pricing strategy in which a hotel sets the rate of its rooms to be the same as its competitive set leader in the area.*

Internal reports *are reports generated in a hotel or lodging establishment with the help of PMS or other systems to show the performance of the establishment in regard to the occupancy rate, ADR, RevPAR, etc.*

Occupancy forecast *refers to the number of rooms estimated to be sold.*

Occupancy rate *refers to the percentage of rooms sold, which can be computed by dividing the number of rooms sold by the total number of rooms available in the hotel for sale.*

Prestige pricing *is a pricing strategy in which a hotel sets the rate of its rooms to be the highest rate in a particular area and justifies the rate with a better product and/or services.*

Rack rate *is the price per room type at which the lodging establishment sells each room when no discounts are offered to any guest.*

Revenue *is a term that refers to the total sales.*

Revenue management (RM) *is a tactical approach used to maximize revenues while supplying the same quantity of product.*

Revenue manager *refers to an individual who manages the tactics used to maximize revenues.*

Revenue management meeting *is a meeting of an organization's department heads with the purpose of enhancing the organization's revenue management philosophy and garnering the support of concerned departments and employees.*

Revenue management team *refers to individuals who manage the tactics used to maximize revenues.*

> **RevPAR** *stands for revenue per available room, which can be computed by dividing rooms' revenue by the total number of rooms available in the hotel for sale.*
>
> **Supply** *refers to the number of rooms available for sale.*

Summary

Revenue management (RM), which could also be referred to as yield management, is a tactical approach used to maximize revenues while supplying the same quantity of product. One of the benefits of revenue management is that it helps enhance revenue and maximize profit.

Rack rate is the price per room when no discounts are offered to any guest. The Hubbart room rate formula and Ogbeide's desired profit rate (ODPR) method offer an objective approach to establishing rack rates. Other methods used for establishing rates include prestige pricing, follow the leader pricing, and check around competitive pricing.

The goal of the revenue manager is to establish a rate that will help maximize RevPAR. An effective revenue manager should continually utilize the essential elements of revenue management (occupancy rate, special event rate, rate discount management, group rate, negotiated rates, and low/high demand tactics) to make decisions in regard to revenue and profit maximization.

Revenue maximization requires decision-making skills of the revenue manager and the efforts of all hotel employees. In addition, the following factors could negatively affect the hotel's RevPAR: (1) poor sales and marketing effort, (2) inadequate room cleanliness, (3) unappealing brand or franchise, (4) poor property access and/or exterior signage, (5) poor decorations and furnishings, (6) poor facility maintenance, (7) inadequate distribution channels, and (8) lack of adequate employees' support.

Keywords and Concepts

ADR

ADR Index

Check Around Competitive Pricing

Close to Arrival (CTA)

Competitive Set

Demand

Early Departure

External Reports

Follow the Leader Pricing

Internal Reports

Minimum Length of Stay (MLOS)

No-Shows

Occupancy Forecast

Occupancy Index

Occupancy Rate

Prestige Pricing

Rack Rate

Revenue

Revenue Management (RM)

Revenue Manager

Revenue Management Meeting

Revenue Management Team

RevPAR

RevPAR Index

Stay-Overs

Supply

The Law of Demand

The Law of Supply

Review Questions

Scenario: As the revenue manager (RM) of a 500-room Charley's resort, you have been asked to maximize the resort's revenue via room sales for the next fiscal year. After analyzing many factors that could affect the resort's revenue and the current trends in the industry, you discovered that the resort's ADR index and the RevPAR index are less than 100 percent, but its occupancy index is around 100 percent. In addition, you also noticed that your average rack rate is 10 percent less than most of your competitive set hotels' and resorts' rack rates. To top it off, Charley's resort is the least promoted lodging establishment compared with its competitive sets.

Consequently, you decided to call a revenue management meeting to inform the general manager and the rest of management about your discovery. By the end of the meeting, it was agreed to keep the monthly occupancy forecast the same as last year's forecast, increase sales and marketing efforts, and increase last year's monthly rates by 10 percent to offset inflation and remain competitive. The monthly actual occupancy rate and ADR for last year are shown below:

Last Year's Occupancy Rate and ADR

	Occupancy Rate (%)	ADR ($)
January	60	195
February	65	210
March	85	250
April	70	210
May	78	250
June	85	250
July	85	250
August	80	250
September	75	250
October	75	230
November	70	210
December	65	195

Questions:

1. What is last year's number of rooms sold?
2. What is last year's revenue?
3. What is the next fiscal year's projected number of rooms to be sold?
4. What is the next fiscal year's projected revenue?
5. What is the difference between the last year's and the next fiscal year's revenue?
6. What is last year's annual occupancy rate?
7. What is last year's ADR?
8. What is last year's RevPAR?
9. What is the next fiscal year's annual occupancy rate?
10. What is the next fiscal year's ADR?
11. What is the next fiscal year's RevPAR?
12. List some factors that could affect the resort's revenue?
13. What would you do in this scenario if your ADR index is less than 100 percent but your RevPAR index and occupancy index are around 100 percent? Would you increase your monthly ADR by 10 percent? Why or why not?
14. What would you do in this scenario if your RevPAR index is less than 100 percent but your ADR index is around 100 percent? Would you increase your monthly ADR by 10 percent? Why or why not? What other factors that could affect the resort's RevPAR would you enhance?
15. What could possibly be the reason(s) why Charley's resort did not achieve an occupancy rate of 100 percent when its average rack rate is 10 percent less than most of its competitive sets, coupled with the fact that its ADR index and the RevPAR index were less than 100 percent?

CHAPTER EIGHT

Cost Control

Learning Objectives

After studying this chapter, you should be able to:

1. Describe the concept of cost.
2. Understand and describe the principles of cost control.
3. Demonstrate the knowledge of beverage cost control.
4. Demonstrate the knowledge of food cost control.
5. Demonstrate the knowledge of labor cost control.
6. Explain other cost-control issues.
7. Use the spreadsheet-modeling approach for cost control.

What is Cost

Cost can be described as an expense incurred by an organization for the production of goods or for services rendered. In food service organizations, the cost of food is incurred when the food is used for the purpose for which it was purchased or when the food is lost due to spoilage or pilfering. Similarly, labor cost is incurred when employees are on duty, regardless of whether they are working or not. There are various types of costs associated with the hospitality industry such as fixed cost, variable cost, food and beverage cost, unit cost, labor cost, prime cost, and controllable and non-controllable cost.

Fixed Costs

Fixed costs are expenses that remain the same regardless of the sales volume. In other words, fixed costs are unaffected by changes in sales volume. Examples of fixed costs include lease on a building, management salaries, and real estate taxes. These costs are fixed because they do not generally increase or decrease with increases or decreases in sales. Using one of the examples above, consider that management salaries for your organization total $100,000 each year. Even if your organization did not produce any goods or render any services, management would still be paid $100,000. Similarly, if your organization's output is more than $1 million, management would still be paid $100,000. Thus, fixed cost is not directly related to the sales volume (output) of the business.

Variable Costs

Variable costs, unlike fixed costs, are expenses that vary with changes in output. In other words, variable costs are affected by changes in sales volume. Variable costs increase with increases in output and decrease with decreases in output. Examples of variable cost are food cost, beverage cost, employees' wages, and some operating expenses (i.e., marketing, utility, cleaning services, guest supplies, etc.). Unlike fixed costs, variable costs are directly related to the output of the business. Some variable costs, however, can only rise as much as the organization allows them to rise. For example, if a food service organization has room for only ten employees to achieve its desired output, even if output continues to increase beyond the desired volume the variable cost (employees' wages) cannot increase beyond the available limit.

Unit Costs

Unit cost is the expenses associated with a portion of food, beverage, or labor. The cost of one chicken breast is a unit cost of chicken breast. Similarly, the cost of one beer, the hourly rate of a cook, and the cost of a portion of fish are all examples of unit cost. The concept of unit costs can be illustrated with a food service organization that purchased a case of chicken breasts for twenty-four dollars. If there are twenty-four chicken breasts per case, the unit cost of each chicken breast is one dollar ($24 ÷ 24). It is very important for effective managers to know unit costs when establishing menu prices and for controlling the profitability of the organization.

"Beware of the little expenses; a small leak will sink a great ship."
Benjamin Franklin
(American statesman, scientist, philosopher, printer, writer, and inventor. 1706–1790)

Total Costs

Total cost is the combination of all unit costs in a given period (i.e., week, month, or year). Total cost can also be described as the sum of variable and fixed costs. Total cost can be used in different forms such as in the total cost of an item (i.e., the total cost of chicken breasts, the total cost of potatoes, total cost of food, and total cost of labor) or as the total cost of production. The concept of total costs can also be illustrated with a food service organization that purchased five cases of chicken breasts for twenty-four dollars per case. If all the cases were consumed in a week, the total cost of chicken breasts for that week is one hundred twenty dollars ($24 × 5). Just like the unit cost, it is important for effective managers to pay close attention to the operation's total costs for the purpose of controlling the profitability of the organization.

Food and Beverage Costs

Food and beverage costs are the expenses incurred by an organization for the purchase of the food and beverage needed for that business. The food and beverage costs include the costs associated with the food and beverage sold, wasted/spilled, compensation, and stolen. Food and beverage costs are among the major responsibilities of food service managers that require critical control and adequate monitoring. Maintaining reasonable food and beverage costs could be a determining factor whether a food service organization makes a profit or loss.

Labor Cost

Labor cost is the sum of salaries and wages paid to employees including employee benefits and payroll taxes. Labor cost is a major cost of doing business in any industry. When establishing the price of goods to be sold or services to be rendered, effective managers usually take labor cost into consideration in addition to other costs of production. Just as food and beverage costs, labor costs require critical control and adequate monitoring. In addition, maintaining reasonable labor costs could be another determining factor whether a food service organization sees a profit or loss.

Prime Cost

Prime cost in the hospitality industry refers to the sum of food cost, beverage cost, and payroll and related expenses. The ability to control prime cost to its lowest level plays an important role in enhancing organizations' financial performance.

"Those who attend to small expenses are always rich."
John Adams
America's 2nd president (1797–1801), 1735–1826

Controllable and Non-Controllable Costs

Some costs are referred to as **controllable costs** because they can be changed in the short term. In contrast, some costs are referred to as **non-controllable** or **uncontrollable costs** because they cannot be changed in the short term. In general, variable costs are good examples of controllable costs. For example, the cost of hourly employee wages can be changed as often as necessary depending on the volume of business. It is not uncommon for food service managers to reduce the number of hourly employees when the business is slow or to ask some employees to stay longer when the organization is very busy. Similarly, an organization might decide to hire more employees or lay off some employees depending on the condition of the organization's business. Food and beverage costs are other good examples of controllable costs; food and beverage costs can be changed by changing the recipe's ingredients, portion size, or by better monitoring to curtail waste and theft.

In contrast with variable costs, fixed costs are good examples of non-controllable costs. For example, the cost of leasing a building cannot be changed by the food service manager due to their wishes over a short-term response to a business's performance. The lease on a building is an example of fixed costs that remain the same for the period of the lease contract. Similarly, management salaries are examples of a non-controllable cost because no matter how slow or busy an organization, management salaries will remain the same. Furthermore, managers on salary cannot be asked to leave their duty early to save labor costs. It doesn't matter if the managers on salary leave early or stay later, their salary will remain the same for that period.

The Concept of Control

Control can be described as the ability to exercise authority over something, somebody, or a situation in order to attain the anticipated goals. Control is a major part of all organizations associated with the planning and establishment of goals, objectives, and standards of an organization including the appropriate rules, policies, and procedures needed to accomplish the organizational standards. Appropriate control within an organization brings about efficiency and effectiveness coupled with the fact that organizational standards will be met with legal correctness.

Management without the necessary control can be compared to our government without the necessary power to act in the best interests of our community, state, or country. For example, if government cannot enact a law against driving while intoxicated, the incidents of accidental deaths due to drunken drivers will be higher than it is today. Similarly, an organization without policies on portion control may be faced with substantial wastes and higher than necessary costs of production. All effective organizations have a control system in all the critical parts of their operations. In the food service industry for example, effective food service organizations have a control system for food purchasing, receiving, storing, issuing, preparation, and service quality.

Management's ability to implement control means that there are rules, policies, and procedures that members of the organization must follow to attain the anticipated goals of the organization. Effective control of an organization is usually based on the ability of management to do the following:

1. Establish standard operating procedures.
2. Train employees to follow the established standards.
3. Monitor and evaluate performance in relation to the established standards.
4. If there is any gap, take the necessary action to meet the established standards.
5. Motivate employees to maintain the established standards.

Obviously, all the above factors of effective organizational control are important. Management, however, must be very careful and rational when it comes to the fourth factor, which is "if there is any gap, take the necessary action to meet the established standards," and the fifth factor, which is "motivate employees to maintain the established standards."

The fourth factor is very significant in regard to correcting errors or deviations that could impede the ability to attain the established standards. Management's corrective actions must be carefully designed to help deviated employees meet the established standards and to discourage other employees from deviating from the established standards. Sometimes the necessary corrective actions apart from training and development might include disciplinary actions, including termination.

Similarly, the fifth factor is very significant in ensuring that splendid and effective employees remain motivated to continue to meet the established standards. It is especially necessary for managers to recognize or award such employees to help ensure they remain motivated to meet or even exceed the established standards. Now that the concept of control has been covered, what is cost control? The following paragraph will be used to cover cost control and the three major areas of control in the food service systems (food, beverage, and labor) that require effective cost control by management.

Cost Control

Cost control is among the major responsibilities of management functions that can have a large impact on the financial performance of an organization. **Cost control** can be described as the process of monitoring costs to attain the anticipated financial goal of the organization. In the food service industry, cost control is a continuous monitoring process that requires strict adherence to the standard of purchasing, receiving, storing, issuing, preparation, and service quality. The cost-control approach may vary from one organization to another, but the purpose of cost control remains the same for all organizations.

"Look everywhere you can to cut a little bit from your expenses. It will all add up to a meaningful sum."

Susan Lynn "Suze" Orman

American author, financial advisor, motivational speaker, and television host

---

Food and Beverage Cost Control

Food and beverage (F&B) cost control is the process of monitoring F&B costs to attain the anticipated financial performance from F&B sales. Just as in most cost-control situations, F&B cost control is a continuous monitoring process that requires strict adherence to the standard of F&B purchasing, receiving, storing, issuing, preparation, and service quality.

Purchasing Standards

The beginning of F&B cost control is to establish standards for purchasing. Different organizations may have a variety of purchasing standards, but F&B purchasing standards should be established by management before making purchasing decisions. When establishing purchasing standards, management should consider the following questions:

1. Which quality of food and alcoholic beverages are suitable for the anticipated guests?
2. Does the purveyor provide discounts for purchasing large quantities? How much of a discount per quantity?
3. What is the best or the most competitive price for the food and alcoholic beverages to be purchased?

The importance of the above questions cannot be undermined. Management must be sincerely critical and rational when responding to the above questions. The better the management responses are the higher the chances of minimizing the cost of purchasing F&B. In addition, government laws and regulations could also affect the cost of beverages. Hence, it is very important for the person in charge of purchasing alcoholic beverages to be aware of the laws and regulations guiding the beverage industry in the region.

Receiving Standards

The purpose of establishing receiving standards is to ensure that the ordered F&B are delivered as ordered. Management must ensure that F&B deliveries are verified to confirm that the quality, quantity, and the prices of the F&B delivered are as ordered. When establishing receiving standards, management should consider the following issues:

1. The need for up-to-date order-receiving records including the name and signature of the receiver and the storing personnel.
2. The importance of verifying that the quality, quantity, and the prices of the F&B delivered are as ordered.
3. The policies and procedures for incomplete and/or damaged deliveries.
4. The needs for the accountability process between the receiver and the storing personnel to confirm that what was received was actually stored.

It is very important for management to establish an accountability process between the receiver and the storing personnel. In fact, it is not a bad idea for the receiver to be different from the storing personnel, or for two of them to work side-by-side for checks and balances. Management's critical consideration of the above issues will help curtail the incidence of wastes and pilferage that could negatively affect F&B cost.

Storing Standards

The purpose of establishing storing standards is to ensure that the ordered F&B are used appropriately as needed. Management must ensure that F&B storage facilities are in good working order. The storing standard established for storing F&B should adopt the following:

- Stored food must be covered and wrapped to a specified standard.
- Stored food must be properly labeled (including date and time of prep).
- Refrigeration and storage areas must meet standards of cleanliness of the organization.
- Thermometers must be present in refrigerators and freezers at all times.
- Refrigerators and freezers must maintain generally accepted temperature zones.

The temperature zone recommended for cold food storage is 32 degrees to 41 degrees Fahrenheit, and zero degrees Fahrenheit or below for freezer food storage. When establishing storing standards, management should consider the following issues:

1. How to secure F&B against theft and bioterrorism.
2. Organization of the storage facilities to maximize shelf space.
3. Policies and procedures for shelving alcoholic beverages.
4. The importance of proper temperature, humidity, and light in the storage facilities.

All of the above storage issues could negatively affect the cost of F&B if management negates the importance of F&B storing control. An effective storing standard and control will help curtail pilferage, enhance necessary accessibility to F&B, and help preserve the quality of F&B.

Issuing Standards

The purpose of establishing issuing standards is to keep an account of the F&B actually used in the process of production. When establishing issuing standards, management should consider the following:

1. The need for designated issuing personnel per shift.
2. The quantities and/or frequency of the F&B to be issued.
3. The legal regulations in regard to handling beverages.
4. The need for establishing par quantities of alcoholic beverages per bar.
5. The need for an effective requisition system for restocking the bars as needed.

Effective issuing standards will help in both controlling the use of F&B for the right reasons and also in maintaining appropriate record keeping for future purposes.

Preparation Standards

One of the most important parts of F&B cost control is the **preparation standard**, which is the standard procedure for production intended to ensure that each portion of a given product conforms to its standard recipe. Effective preparation standard means that each portion of a given product will be identical to all other portions of the same product. Another standard procedure deemed highly important in the food service industry is the **standard portion size**, or the quantity of a product to be served each time the product is ordered.

The importance of standard portion size cannot be overemphasized when it comes to F&B cost control. Portion size is that aspect of food service operations that is easily abused by employees. Management needs to establish an effective portion-control system to curtail the incidence of too small or too much serving size. When the portion size is too small the customers may be unhappy and complain. If the complaint is bad enough to warrant some form of management compensation, that will increase the cost of that product. Similarly, when the portion size is too large or more than the standard portion size the cost of that product rises, which will then affect the total F&B cost for that period. Management needs to emphasize how important it is for cooks and servers to follow the portion size regularly. Any deviation from the standard portion size of any product will definitely affect the overall F&B cost of the organization. When establishing preparation standard and portion control, management should consider the following:

1. Establish standard procedures and quantities that are realistic and can be easily followed.
2. Provide equipment, tools, or devices for production staff members and servers to meet the appropriate preparation standard and portion size.
3. Establish a shift-by-shift, daily, or weekly inventory system for popular items to help identify product waste or pilferage before it's too late.
4. Train employees appropriately to follow the established standards.
5. Monitor performance in relation to the established standards.

Each of the above considerations requires some form of planning. The extent of the planning depends on the size and the food service concept of the organization. For the preparation standard and portion control to be effective, however, management must be consistent and continuously strive for adherence to the appropriate standards.

Service Quality Standards

Another major part of F&B cost control is to be able to provide good service to the guests at all times without errors or deviation from the organization's quality standard. Any mistake in food or beverage ordered by a guest that results in waste increases F&B cost. Similarly, any employee who intentionally gives away food or beverage for free is increasing F&B cost. For the above reasons, management needs to provide all employees with good and adequate training to help curtail the occurrences of mistakes, and have a monitoring mechanism in place to help supervise employees and discourage them from giving away food and beverage for free.

Labor Cost Control

In the hospitality industry, labor cost is one of the highest expenses in the P&L statement. Labor cost percentage varies from one organization to another. In most hospitality organizations, it is generally between 15–45 percent of the total sales. The ability to control labor cost is critical in regard to the financial performance of any organization. Effective management usually has plans and techniques for controlling labor costs. When establishing plans and techniques governing labor cost control, management and business owners should consider the following factors:

1. **Number of Salary Employees**: The more employees you have on salary, the higher the fixed cost. Unlike hourly wage employees, management cannot reduce the number of employees on salary when business is slow.
2. **Optimum Number of Employees per Shift**: The more employees you have on schedule, the higher your labor cost. It is vital for management to consider potential business volume per shift when scheduling employees. It is not uncommon for some employees to be scheduled on a split shift basis. These employees are scheduled to work a short, busy shift and then leave, and return to do another shift as needed.
3. **Labor Control between Shifts:** Management must be ready and steadfast to reduce the number of employees on duty when business is slow. The lower the sales volume for a constant number of employees, the higher the labor cost percentage.
4. **Number of Full-Time Employees:** The number of full-time employees in the organization could significantly affect the labor cost. More full-time employees generally mean more benefits and payroll taxes, which could translate to more labor cost. Management, however, should refrain from trading two or more employees for the role of a full-time employee just to save labor cost.
5. **Outsourcing:** Some organizations arrange for certain work to be done by an outside organization on a contractual basis instead of hiring additional full-time employees. Management/ business owners should know when to use outsourcing to reduce labor costs.
6. **Business Concept:** The type of business concept utilized can have a severe impact on labor costs. For example, the amount and quality of employees needed for food service operations varies from one food service concept to another. Food service concepts dictate the menu, layout, equipment, preparation methods, service, and hours of operation. More labor hours are generally needed for more complex concepts.

The purpose of labor cost control is to enhance the efficiency of the organization's labor force in a way that will help maximize the financial performance of the organization. The basic idea behind labor cost control is that there should be enough employees in each department to complete the necessary tasks efficiently, but none of the employees should be on duty to stand around with nothing to do.

Other Cost-Control Issues

Some other cost-control issues include other controllable operational expenses such as employee meal discounts, operating supplies, utility cost, advertising and promotion, etc. It's very important for management not to take these operational expenses for granted. Management should continuously analyze its financial statement and monitor the ratio of each cost to revenue (cost percentage). The higher the cost percentage of each of the expenses, the lower the net income. The goal of management in regard to the operational expenses is to budget appropriately to ensure the operational needs are not excessively funded. Employee meal discounts, operating supplies, and utility usage should be continuously monitored by management to prevent them from being abused by employees.

There is no reason for any food service management to complain and do nothing about high operating expenses instead of controlling the following:

1. The ghost flushes in the restrooms.
2. The unnecessary constantly running faucet in the preparation station.
3. Keeping more than one grill and fryer on during a very slow period.
4. Wasting of operating supplies (e.g., to-go plates and cups, condiments, napkins, etc.).
5. Fraudulent use of employee meal discounts, etc.

Effective managers who are sincerely concerned about the financial performance of their organization will pay close attention to each of the above concerns and resolve them appropriately.

"I am indeed rich, since my income is superior to my expenses, and my expense is equal to my wishes."
Edward Gibbon
English historian, 1737–1794

Cost-Control Software and Costs Calculation

There are computer software programs to assist food service management in ordering, receiving, issuing, and keeping track of F&B cost. Some of these programs can keep track of F&B orders, prices of ordered F&B, and inventory balances. And some of them can actually help management in maintaining standard F&B cost by enabling management to easily notice when F&B is wasted or missing. Some examples of common food service software are ChefTec, Comtrex Systems Software Suites, and Meal Cost System. In fact, many point of sale systems can help keep track of inventory balances, etc. But management can also keep track of F&B orders, prices of ordered F&B, and inventory balances without software. Management can keep track of inventory balances manually and keep track of F&B costs regularly via simple calculations. The following paragraph will focus on the calculation of the standard portion cost, cost of F&B issued/consumed, and F&B cost percentage. These formulas will make calculation of the standard portion cost, cost of F&B issued/consumed, and F&B cost percentage a lot easier:

Formulas

8.1. Standard Portion Cost = $\dfrac{\text{Purchase Price Per Unit}}{\text{Number of Portions Per Unit}}$

8.2. Cost of F&B Issued = Opening Inventory + Food Purchase – Closing Inventory

8.3. Food Cost Percentage = $\dfrac{\text{Food Cost}}{\text{Food Sales}} \times 100$

8.4. Beverage Cost Percentage = $\dfrac{\text{Beverage Cost}}{\text{Beverage Sales}} \times 100$

8.5. Labor Cost Percentage = $\dfrac{\text{Labor Cost}}{\text{Revenue (Total Sales)}} \times 100$

EXAMPLE 8.1
Calculating Standard Portion Cost
A case of beer containing twenty-four bottles costs eighteen dollars. If the standard portion of this beer is one bottle, what is the standard portion cost of a bottle of beer?

Using formula 8.1 above: Standard Portion Cost = $\dfrac{\text{Purchase Price Per Unit}}{\text{Number of Portions Per Unit}}$

= **$0.75**

EXAMPLE 8.2
Calculating Cost of F&B Issued/Consumed
If the total cost of the opening inventory at the beginning of the month is $8,500, the cost of food purchases within the month is $24,500, and the cost of the closing inventory at the end of the month is $6,000, what is the cost of F&B issued for that month?

Using Formula 8.2 above:
Cost of F&B Issued = Opening Inventory + Food Purchase – Closing Inventory
= $8,500 + $24,500 – $6,000
= **$27,000**

EXAMPLE 8.3
Calculating Food Cost Percentage
For the purpose of reinforcement, let's use the example from Charley's Kitchen in Example 6.1 (Exhibit 6.1). Charley's Kitchen's food sales in the fiscal year 2012 equals $1,225,000 and the cost of food sold for the same year was $392,000. What was Charley's Kitchen's food cost percentage for fiscal year 2012?

Using Formula 8.3 above: Food Cost Percentage $= \dfrac{\text{Food Cost}}{\text{Food Sales}} \times 100$

$$= \dfrac{\$392{,}000}{\$1{,}225{,}000} \times 100$$

$$= \textbf{32\%}$$

EXAMPLE 8.4
Calculating Beverage Cost Percentage

Again using the example from Charley's Kitchen in Example 6.1 (Exhibit 6.1). Charley's Kitchen beverage sales in fiscal year 2012 equals $75,200 and the cost of beverage sold for the same year was $21,056. What was Charley's Kitchen's beverage cost percentage for fiscal year 2012?

Using Formula 8.4 above: Beverage Cost Percentage $= \dfrac{\text{Beverage Cost}}{\text{Beverage Sales}} \times 100$

$$= \dfrac{\$21{,}056}{\$75{,}200} \times 100$$

$$= \textbf{28\%}$$

Spreadsheet-Modeling Approach For Cost Control

EXAMPLE 8.5
Calculating the Cost of a Banquet Menu

Scenario: As an assistant catering manager at Charley's Kitchen, one of your responsibilities is costing the banquet menu for group events. After agreeing on a menu for an organization's event, the manager of the organization requested a portion cost sheet from you for the event, as shown below:

Items	Portion Cost ($)
Special salad	0.50
Steak (12 oz.)	4.80
Potatoes	0.30
Vegetable	0.50
Special sauce	0.35
Rolls and butter	0.50
Coffee	0.20

After applying the markup for a food cost percentage of 32 you faxed the proposal to the manager of the organization. The manager, however, found the cost per person a little high and asked you to provide him with a lower price after reducing the size of the steak from twelve to eight ounces. Calculate the costs per person with twelve ounces of steak and eight ounces of steak after the markup?

ANSWER: To solve this question, you need to be familiar with some formulas as outlined above (Formulas 8.1–8.4), then use key cell formulas as shown in Exhibit 8.1, as outlined below.

Exhibit 8.1: Spreadsheet-Modeling Approach to Example 8.5

C12 =(C11)/0.32

Costing a Banquet Menu

Items	12 Ounces Steak Portion Costs ($)	8 Ounces Steak Portion Costs ($)
Special Salad	0.50	0.50
Steak (12 oz.)	4.80	**3.20**
Potatoes	0.30	0.30
Vegetable	0.50	0.50
Special Sauce	0.35	0.35
Rolls and butter	0.50	0.50
Coffee	0.20	0.20
Total Cost	$ 7.15	$ 5.55
Cost/guest (at 32% food cos	$ 22.34	$ 17.34

Key Cell Formulas		
Variable	**Cell**	**Formula**
Portion cost of 8 ounces of steak	C5	=(B5/12)*8
Total menu cost (12 oz.)	B11	=SUM(B4:B10)
Total menu cost (8 oz.)	C11	=SUM(C4:C10)
Cost/person after markup (12 oz.)	B12	=B11/0.32
Cost/person after markup (8 oz.)	C12	=C11/0.32

The answer to Example 8.5 is displayed in Exhibit 8.1 above. If your spreadsheet solutions are correct, the following should be the answers:

The cost per person with 12 ounces of steak after the markup = **$22.34**
The cost per person with 8 ounces of steak after the markup = **$17.34**

EXAMPLE 8.6

Scenario: Haley Bailey was hired by a management company as a restaurant manager for a busy restaurant in Bentonville, Arkansas. The restaurant was steadily patronized by business executives affiliated with Wal-Mart Corporation on weekdays and by families and tourists visiting the Crystal Bridges museum on weekends. As a result, the restaurant was relatively very busy throughout the year.

During her interview with the restaurant owner, Haley was given an analysis of the restaurant operations and then asked to help enhance the existing high labor cost problems. The restaurant operation is great, but the owner hoped the organization's labor percentage before payroll benefits and related expenses could be reduced by about 4 percent without damaging the service quality. On Haley's analysis of the restaurant operations, she observed that although the restaurant is relatively busy, it is not busy enough for employees to be scheduled as they were in the previous year. The daily standing schedule for the previous year is shown in Exhibit 8.2 below.

Exhibit 8.2: Previous Year's Scheduled

Employee	Time at work	# of employees
Server	6 a.m.-2 p.m.	2
Server	7 a.m.-11:30 a.m.	4
Server	11 a.m-4 p.m.	2
Server	2 p.m.-10 p.m.	2
Server	5 p.m.-10 p.m.	3
Server	4 p.m.-12 a.m.	2
Cook	6 a.m.-2 p.m.	3
Cook	7 a.m.-11:30 a.m.	1
Cook	11 a.m.-3 p.m.	2
Cook	2 p.m.-10 p.m.	2
Cook	5 p.m.-10 p.m.	3
Cook	4 p.m.-12 a.m.	2

Exhibit 8.3: Next Fiscal Year's Scheduled

Employee	Time at work	# of employees
Server	6 a.m.-2 p.m.	1
Server	8 a.m.-2 p.m.	1
Server	7-11:30 a.m.	2
Server	11 a.m-3 p.m.	3
Server	2-10 p.m.	1
Server	2-8 p.m.	1
Server	5-10 p.m.	2
Server	4 p.m.-12 a.m.	1
Server	4-10 p.m.	1
Cook	6 a.m.-2 p.m.	2
Cook	8 a.m.-2 p.m.	1
Cook	11a.m.-3 p.m.	2
Cook	2-10 p.m.	1
Cook	2–8 p.m.	1
Cook	5-10 p.m.	2
Cook	4 p.m.-12 a.m.	2

Restaurant revenue for the previous year was $1.7 million and management salary was $100,000. The average hourly wage is $4.50 for servers and $8.25 for cooks. Haley worked out the next fiscal year's labor cost for the restaurant, keeping the projected revenue and the management salary the same as last year's. To enhance the labor costs, she modified the standing schedule for the next fiscal year as shown in Exhibit 8.3 below.

Question: Compute the annual labor cost percentage before payroll benefits and related expenses for the two schedules based on the yearly revenue of $1.7 million. What is the difference between the previous and next fiscal year's labor cost percentage points before payroll benefits and related expenses?

ANSWER: To solve this question, you need to be familiar with basic arithmetic skills, labor cost percentage formula as shown in Formula 8.5, remember the spreadsheet design guiding principles in Chapter 1 (as listed in Exhibit 4.3), and then follow the step-by-step, hands-on approach to Example 8.6 as outlined below.

STEP-BY-STEP, HANDS-ON APPROACH TO EXAMPLE 8.6

1. In your Excel spreadsheet, start with the headings by inserting *Previous Year's Scheduled Labor Cost Percentage* in cell B1.
2. Following the above heading, insert *Employee, Time at Work, # of Hours, # of Employees, Rate / Hour*, and *Cost/Year* in cells A2, B2, C2, D2, E2, and F2, respectively.
3. Insert servers below the *Employee* heading in cells A3–A8 (see below).

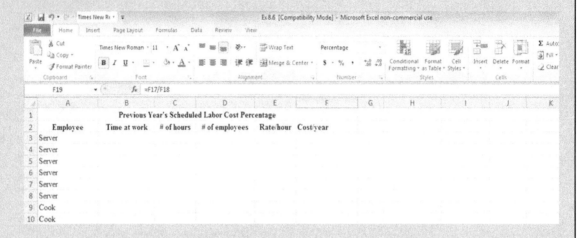

4. Similarly, inserts cooks below the *Employee* heading immediately following the servers in cells A9–A14.
5. Inserts the given time at work (see Exhibit 8.2) corresponding to the servers and cooks below the *Time at Work* heading in cells B5–B14.
6. Insert the number of hours worked per day below the *# of Hours* heading in cells C3–C14.
7. Insert the number of employees per each time at work below the *# of Employees* heading in cells D3–D14.
8. Insert the rate per hour for the servers and cooks below the *Rate/Hour* heading in cells E3–E14.
9. Compute the cost of labor for each group of servers and cooks per year below the *Cost/Year* heading in cells F3–F14. Using the following formula:

$$\text{Cost/Year} = \left\{\begin{array}{c}\text{\# of} \\ \text{Hours}\end{array}\right\} \times \left\{\begin{array}{c}\text{\# of} \\ \text{Employees}\end{array}\right\} \times \{\text{Rate/Hour}\} \times \{365\}$$

10. *To compute the cost of labor for each group of servers and cooks per year*, select the cell in which you want to place the formula (i.e., F3).
11. Type an equal sign (=) to start the formula. Click the first cell you want to place in the formula (i.e., C3). When you click the cell, a border surrounds the cell indicating the cell you are working with and its name appears on the formula bar. Next, type the asterisk (*) key to the formula bar to form [=C3*]. Click the second cell you want to place in the formula (i.e., D3) to form [=C3*D3].
12. Next, type the asterisk (*) key to the formula bar to form [=C3*D3*]. Click the third cell you want to place in the formula (i.e., E3) to form [=C3*D3*E3].

13. Next, type the asterisk (*) key to the formula bar to form [=C3*D3*E3*]. Then insert 365 in the formula bar to form [=C3*D3*E3*365].

14. Then press the enter key. Excel calculates the result and displays it in the cell as **$26,280**.

15. *To compute the number of rooms sold per day for the rest of the months*, just copy cell F3 ($26,280) and paste in each of the other cells below the *Cost/Year* heading.

16. If cell F3 ($26,280) is copied and pasted correctly into cells F4–F14 for the automatic computation of the rest of the employees' labor cost/year, you should have the following: F4 = $29,565.00; F5 = $16,425.00; F6 = ($26,280); ... F14 = $48,180.

17. Now you can compute the hourly employees' labor cost per year in cell F15.

18. *To compute the hourly employees' labor cost per year*, select the cell in which you want to place the formula (i.e., F15).

19. Type an equal sign (=) to start the formula. Since you are adding more than two variables, you could use the sum function to make it faster. Hence, type in SUM after the equal sign (=) followed with an open parenthesis to form [=SUM( ]. Select the cells you want to sum up in the formula (i.e., F3:F14). When you select the cells, a border surrounds the cells indicating the cell you are summing up, which will appear on the formula bar. Next, insert the close parenthesis to form [=SUM(F3:F14)], then press the enter key. Excel calculates the result and displays it in the cell as **$400,906.88**.

20. Now insert the management salary in cell F16 ($100,000), then compute the total labor cost before payroll benefit and related expenses.

21. *To compute the total labor cost before payroll benefits and related expenses*, type an equal sign (=) to start the formula in cell F17. Click the first cell you want to place in the formula (i.e., F15). When you click the cell, a border surrounds the cell indicating the cell you are working with and its name appears on the formula bar. Next, type the plus (+) key to the formula bar to form [=F15+]. Click the second cell you want to place in the formula (i.e., F16) to form [=F15+F16], then press the enter key. Excel calculates the result and displays it in the cell as **$500,906.88**.

22. Then insert the given annual revenue in cell F18 ($1,700,000).

23. Then select the cell in which you want to place the *Previous Year's Annual Labor Cost Percentage* (i.e., F19).

24. Type an equal sign (=) to start the formula. Click the first cell you want to place in the formula (i.e., F17).

25. Next, type the slash" (/) key to the formula bar to form [=F17/]. Click the second cell you want to place in the formula (i.e., F18) to form [=F17/F18], then press the enter key. Excel calculates the result and displays it in the cell as **0.2947**.

26. Click the percentage (%) sign in the Excel tool bar. Excel calculates the result and displays it in the cell. If you limit your result to two decimal places you will have **29.47%**.

27. Now that you are done computing the previous year's annual labor cost percentage, you are ready *to compute the next fiscal year's annual labor cost percentage*.

28. In your Excel spreadsheet, start with the headings by inserting *Next Fiscal Year's Scheduled Labor Cost Percentage* in cell B22.

29. Following the above heading, insert *Employee, Time at Work, # of hours, # of Employees, Rate/Hour*, and *Cost/Year* in cells A23, B23, C23, D23, E23, and F23, respectively.

30. Insert servers below the *Employee* heading in cells A24–A32 (see below).

	A	B	C	D	E	F	G	H	I	J	K
15	Hourly Employees' Labor Cost					$ 400,906.88					
16	Management Labor Cost					$ 100,000.00					
17	Total Labor Cost					$ 500,906.88					
18	Revenue					$ 1,700,000.00					
19	Previous Year's Annual Labor Cost Percentage					29.47%					
20											
21											
22			New Fiscal Year's Labor Cost Percentage								
23	Employee	Time at work	# of hours	# of employees	Rate/hour	Cost/year					
24	Server										
25	Server										
26	Server										
27	Server										
28	Server										
29	Server										
30	Server										
31	Server										
32	Server										
33	Cook										
34	Cook										

31. Similarly, insert "Cook" below the *Employee* heading immediately following the servers in cells A33–A39.
32. Insert the given time at work (see Exhibit 8.3) corresponding to the servers and cooks below the *Time at Work* heading in cells B24–B39.
33. Insert the number of hours worked per day below the *# of Hours* heading in cells C24–C39.
34. Insert the number of employees per each time at work below the *# of Employees* heading in cells D24–D39.
35. Insert the rate per hour for the servers and cooks below the *Rate/Hour* heading in cells E24–E39.
36. Compute the cost of labor for each group of servers and cooks per year below the *Cost/Year* heading in cells F24–F39. Using the following formula:

$$\text{Cost/Year} = \left\{ \begin{matrix} \# \text{ of} \\ \text{Hours} \end{matrix} \right\} \times \left\{ \begin{matrix} \# \text{ of} \\ \text{Employees} \end{matrix} \right\} \times \{\text{Rate/Hour}\} \times \{365\}$$

37. To compute the cost of labor for each group of servers and cooks per year, select the cell in which you want to place the formula (i.e., F24).
38. Type an equal sign (=) to start the formula. Click the first cell you want to place in the formula (i.e., C24). When you click the cell, a border surrounds the cell indicating the cell you are working with and its name appears on the formula bar. Next, type the asterisk (*) key to the formula bar to form [=C24*]. Click the second cell you want to place in the formula (i.e., D24) to form [=C24*D24].
39. Next, type the asterisk (*) key to the formula bar to form [=C24*D24*]. Click the third cell you want to place in the formula (i.e., E24) to form [=C24*D24*E24].
40. Next, type the asterisk (*) key to the formula bar to form [=C24*D24*E24*]. Then insert 365 in the formula bar to form [=C24*D24*E24*365].
41. Then press the enter key. Excel calculates the result and displays it in the cell as **$13,140**.

42. *To compute the number of rooms sold per day for the rest of the months,* just copy cell F24 ($13,140) and paste in each of the other cells below the *Cost/Year* heading.

43. If cell F24 ($13,140) is copied and pasted correctly into cells F25–F39 for the automatic computation of the rest of the employees' labor cost/year, you should have the following: F25 = $9,855; F26 = $14,782.50; F27 = ($19,710); . . . F39 = $48,180.

44. Now you can compute the hourly employees' labor cost per year in cell F40.

45. *To compute the hourly employees labor cost per year,* select the cell in which you want to place the formula (i.e., F40).

46. Type an equal sign (=) to start the formula. Since you are adding more than two variables, you could use the sum function to make it faster. Hence, type in SUM after the equal sign (=) followed with an open parenthesis to form [=SUM( ]. Select the cells you want to sum up in the formula (i.e., F24:F39). When you select the cells, a border surrounds the cells indicating the cell you are summing up, which will appear on the formula bar. Next, insert the close parenthesis to form [=SUM(F24:F39)], then press the enter key. Excel calculates the result and displays it in the cell as **$330,690**.

47. Now insert the management salary in cell F41 ($100,000), then compute the total labor cost before payroll benefits and related expenses.

48. *To compute the total labor cost before payroll benefits and related expenses,* type an equal sign (=) to start the formula in cell F42. Click the first cell you want to place in the formula (i.e., F40). When you click the cell, a border surrounds the cell indicating the cell you are working with and its name appears on the formula bar. Next, type the plus (+) key to the formula bar to form [=F40+]. Click the second cell you want to place in the formula (i.e., F41) to form [=F40+F41], then press the enter key. Excel calculates the result and displays it in the cell as **$430,690**.

49. Then insert the given annual revenue in cell F43 ($1,700,000).

50. Then select the cell in which you want to place the *Previous Year's Annual Labor Cost Percentage* (i.e., F44).

51. Type an equal sign (=) to start the formula. Click the first cell you want to place in the formula (i.e., F42).

52. Next, type the slash (/) key to the formula bar to form [=F42/]. Click the second cell you want to place in the formula (i.e., F43) to form [=F42/F43], then press the enter key. Excel calculates the result and displays it in the cell as **0.2533**.

53. Click the percentage (%) sign in the Excel tool bar. Excel calculates the result and displays it in the cell. If you limit your result to two decimal places you will have **25.33%**.

54. Now that you are done computing the previous year's annual labor cost percentage and the next fiscal year's annual labor cost percentage, it is time to compute the difference in both annual labor cost percentages.

55. *To compute the Differences in Both Annual Labor Cost Percentages,* select the cell in which you want to place the formula (i.e., F46).

56. Type an equal sign (=) to start the formula. Click the first cell you want to place in the formula (i.e., F19). When you click the cell, a border surrounds the cell indicating the cell you are working with and its name appears on the formula bar. Next, type the minus" (−) key to the formula bar to form [=F19−].

57. Click the second cell you want to place in the formula (i.e., F44) to form [=F19−F44], then press the enter key. Excel calculates the result and displays it in the cell as **4.13%**.

Exhibit 8.4: Previous Year's Annual Labor Cost Percentage

F44 =F42/F43

	A	B	C	D	E	F
1	**Previous Year's Scheduled Labor Cost Percentage**					
2	**Employee**	**Time at work**	**# of hours**	**# of employees**	**Rate/hour**	**Cost/year**
3	Server	6am - 2 pm	8	2	$ 4.50	$ 26,280.00
4	Server	7am - 11:30pm	4.5	4	$ 4.50	$ 29,565.00
5	Server	11am - 4pm	5	2	$ 4.50	$ 16,425.00
6	Server	2pm - 10pm	8	2	$ 4.50	$ 26,280.00
7	Server	5pm - 10pm	5	3	$ 4.50	$ 24,637.50
8	Server	4pm - 12am	8	2	$ 4.50	$ 26,280.00
9	Cook	6am - 2 pm	8	3	$ 8.25	$ 72,270.00
10	Cook	7am - 11:30am	4.5	1	$ 8.25	$ 13,550.63
11	Cook	11am - 3pm	4	2	$ 8.25	$ 24,090.00
12	Cook	2pm - 10pm	8	2	$ 8.25	$ 48,180.00
13	Cook	5pm - 10pm	5	3	$ 8.25	$ 45,168.75
14	Cook	4pm - 12am	8	2	$ 8.25	$ 48,180.00
15	**Hourly Employees' Labor Cost**					**$ 400,906.88**
16	Management Labor Cost					$ 100,000.00
17	**Total Labor Cost**					**$ 500,906.88**
18	**Revenue**					**$ 1,700,000.00**
19	**Previous Year's Annual Labor Cost Percentage**					**29.47%**
20						

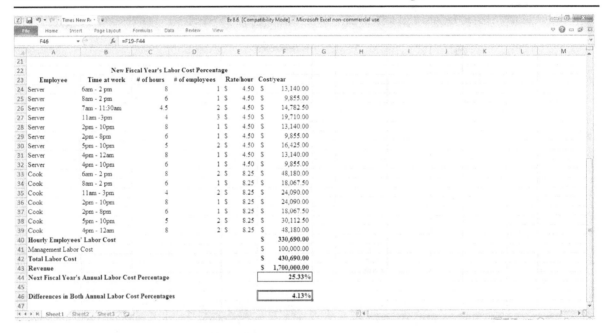

Exhibit 8.5: Next Fiscal Year's Annual Labor Cost Percentage

F46 =F19-F44

	A	B	C	D	E	F
21						
22	**New Fiscal Year's Labor Cost Percentage**					
23	**Employee**	**Time at work**	**# of hours**	**# of employees**	**Rate/hour**	**Cost/year**
24	Server	6am - 2 pm	8	1	$ 4.50	$ 13,140.00
25	Server	8am - 2 pm	6	1	$ 4.50	$ 9,855.00
26	Server	7am - 11:30am	4.5	2	$ 4.50	$ 14,782.50
27	Server	11am -3pm	4	3	$ 4.50	$ 19,710.00
28	Server	2pm - 10pm	8	1	$ 4.50	$ 13,140.00
29	Server	2pm - 8pm	6	1	$ 4.50	$ 9,855.00
30	Server	5pm - 10pm	5	2	$ 4.50	$ 16,425.00
31	Server	4pm - 12am	8	1	$ 4.50	$ 13,140.00
32	Server	4pm - 10pm	6	1	$ 4.50	$ 9,855.00
33	Cook	6am - 2 pm	8	2	$ 8.25	$ 48,180.00
34	Cook	8am - 2 pm	6	1	$ 8.25	$ 18,067.50
35	Cook	11am - 3pm	4	2	$ 8.25	$ 24,090.00
36	Cook	2pm - 10pm	8	1	$ 8.25	$ 24,090.00
37	Cook	2pm - 8pm	6	1	$ 8.25	$ 18,067.50
38	Cook	5pm - 10pm	5	2	$ 8.25	$ 30,112.50
39	Cook	4pm - 12am	8	2	$ 8.25	$ 48,180.00
40	**Hourly Employees' Labor Cost**					**$ 330,690.00**
41	Management Labor Cost					$ 100,000.00
42	**Total Labor Cost**					**$ 430,690.00**
43	**Revenue**					**$ 1,700,000.00**
44	**Next Fiscal Year's Annual Labor Cost Percentage**					**25.33%**
45						
46	**Differences in Both Annual Labor Cost Percentages**					**4.13%**
47						

By following the above instructions you should be done computing the *Previous Year's Annual Labor Cost Percentage*, the *Next Fiscal Year's Annual Labor Cost Percentage*, and the *Difference Between Both Annual Labor Cost Percentages.* If you make any mistakes when typing any of the numbers, do not panic. Just make the necessary changes and all the calculations will be automatically corrected. The results of the spreadsheet-modeling approach to Example 8.6 are displayed below in Exhibits 8.4 and 8.5.

ACCOUNTING AND FINANCIAL TERMINOLOGY

Cost *is an expense incurred by an organization for the production of goods or for services rendered.*

Cost control *is the process of monitoring costs in order to attain the anticipated financial goal of the organization.*

Control *is the ability to exercise authority over something, somebody, or a situation in order to attain the anticipated goals.*

Controllable costs *are cost that can be changed in the short term.*

Fiscal year *is the twelve-month accounting period used by business organizations.*

Fixed costs *are expenses that remain the same regardless of the sales volume. In other words, fixed costs are unaffected by changes in sales volume.*

Food and beverage costs *are the expenses incurred by an organization for the purchase of the food and beverage needed for that business.*

Food and beverage (F&B) cost control *is the process of monitoring F&B costs in order to attain the anticipated financial performance from F&B sales.*

Labor cost *is the sum of salaries and wages paid to employees including employee benefits and payroll taxes.*

Non-controllable or **uncontrollable costs** *are costs that cannot be changed in the short term.*

Preparation standard *is the standard procedure for production intended to ensure that each portion of a given product conforms to its standard recipe.*

Prime cost *in the hospitality industry refers to the sum of food cost, beverage cost, and payroll and related expenses.*

Revenue *is a term that refers to the total sales.*

Standard portion size *refers to the quantity of a product to be served each time the product is ordered.*

Total cost *is the combination of all unit costs in a given period (i.e., week, month, or year). Total cost can also be described as the sum of variable and fixed costs.*

Unit cost *is the expenses associated with a portion of food, beverage, or labor.*

Variable costs *are expenses that vary with changes in output. In other words, variable costs are affected by changes in sales volume.*

Summary

Cost control is the process of monitoring costs to attain the anticipated financial goal of an organization. In most industries, cost control is a continuous monitoring process, which requires strict adherence to the organization's standard operating procedures in order to curtail unnecessary waste and expenses.

The main purpose of food, beverage, and labor cost control is to enhance the efficiency of organizations in a way that will help maximize their financial success. Effective cost-control measures should be based on management's ability to do the following:

1. Establish standard operating procedures.
2. Train employees to follow the established standards.
3. Monitor and evaluate performance in relation to the established standards.
4. If there is any gap, take the necessary action to meet the established standards.
5. Motivate employees to maintain the established standards.

Keywords and Concepts

Cost

Cost Control

Control

Controllable Costs

Fiscal Year

Fixed Costs

Food and Beverage (F&B) Costs

Food and Beverage (F&B) Cost Control

Labor Cost

Non-controllable or Uncontrollable Costs

Preparation Standard

Prime Cost

Revenue

Standard Portion Size

Total Cost

Unit Cost

Variable Costs

Review Questions

1. What is the cost percentage of each of the following cost if the total sales equal $2,500? Round your answers to the nearest two decimal figures.
   A. Cost = $150
   B. Cost = $200
   C. Cost = $250
   D. Cost = $300
   E. Cost = $500
   F. Cost = $600

2. What is the equivalent cost of each of the following cost percentages if the total sales equal $5,000? Round your answers to the nearest two decimal figures.
   A. Cost percentages = 35%
   B. Cost percentages = 30%
   C. Cost percentages = 25%
   D. Cost percentages = 20%
   E. Cost percentages = 15%
   F. Cost percentages = 10%

3. What is the sales value for each of the following, given the following values of costs and cost percentages? Round your answers to the nearest two decimal figures.
   A. Cost percentage = 30%; Cost = $600
   B. Cost percentages = 25%; Cost = $750
   C. Cost percentages = 20%; Cost = $1,000
   D. Cost percentages = 15%; Cost = $1,500
   E. Cost percentages = 10%; Cost = $2,000
   F. Cost percentages = 5%; Cost = $2,500

4. Charley's Kitchen purchases domestic red wine at ten dollars per bottle. Each bottle contains one hundred ounces of wine. If the standard portion size of the wine is five ounces (one glass), solve the following:
   A. What is the standard portion cost?
   B. What is the total cost of sixty glasses of wine?
   C. If Charley's Kitchen served two hundred guests at a banquet, with each guest served one glass of this domestic red wine.
      I. How many bottles were served?
      II. What is the cost of wine served?
      III. If the markup on the cost of each glass is 25 percent, what is the cost of a standard portion size?

5. The following information was prepared by the manager of Charley's Kitchen. The information is the projection of the sales and various costs for the next fiscal year.

Food sales = $850,000
Beverage sales = $250,000
Cost of food = 28 percent of food sales
Cost of beverages = 24 percent of beverage sales
Hourly employees' wages: 20 percent of revenue
Management salaries = 5 percent of revenue

   Using this information, compute the following variables?
   A. What is the revenue?
   B. What is the cost of food?

C. What is the cost of beverage?

D. What are the hourly employees' labor cost?

E. What is the management salary?

F. What is the total labor cost?

References

Dopson, L. R. and Hayes, D. K. (2009). *Managerial Accounting for the Hospitality Industry*. New Jersey: John Wiley & Sons, Inc.

Gregoire, M. B. (2010). *Foodservice Organization: A Management and Systems Approach, 6th Edition*. Upper Saddle River, New Jersey: Pearson-Prentice Hall.

Hayes, D. K., Ninemeier, J. D., and Miller, A. A. (2012). *Foundations of Lodging Management, 2nd Edition*. Upper Saddle River, New Jersey: Pearson-Prentice Hall.

Investopedia (2013). *Accounting (Fundamental Analysis) Terms*. Retrieved January 4th 2013. http://www.investopedia.com/categories/accounting.asp?page=1

Meigs, R. F., Meigs, M. A., Mark, B., and Whittington, A. (1996). *Accounting: The basis for Business Decisions, 10th Edition*. The McGraw-Hill Companies, Inc.

Morse, D. C., and Zimmerman, J. (1997). *Managerial Accounting*. Irwin Book Team: The McGraw-Hill Companies, Inc.

Professional Meeting Management (2006). *Comprehensive Strategies for Meetings, Conventions and Events*. Dubuque, Iowa: Kendall/Hunt Publishing Company.

QFinance (2013). *Finance and Business Quotes*. Retrieved January 4th 2013. http://www.qfinance.com/finance-and-business-quotes

Ragsdale, C. T. (1998). *Spreadsheet Modeling and Decision Analysis*. Cincinnati, Ohio: South-Western College Publishing.

Woods, R. H., Ninemeier, J. D., Hayes, D. K., and Austin, M. A. (2007). *Professional Front Office Management, 1st Edition*. Upper Saddle River, New Jersey: Pearson-Prentice Hall.

Glossary

Accelerated depreciation *is a method of depreciation that recognizes larger amounts of the asset's cost as depreciation expense in the early years and declining amounts in the subsequent years over the estimated useful life of the asset.*

Accounting *is basically a system for compiling and reporting an organization's monetary information for making economic decisions.*

Accounting system *includes the procedures, devices, personnel, and other records used by an organization to develop accounting information and reporting the information to decision makers.*

Accounts payable *are the amounts a business entity owes for items or services purchased on credit without a promissory note that needs to be paid within a year.*

Accounts receivable *is the value of the money that is yet to be collected for providing products and/ or services to customers.*

ADR *stands for average daily rate, which can be computed by dividing rooms' revenue by the number of rooms sold.*

Annual operating budgets *are thorough projections of revenue and expenses based on a rationally forecasted sale of products and/or services during a specified period (usually one year).*

Annual report *is a document issued annually to the public to help stakeholders and potential stakeholders evaluate the organization's past performance, and to make plans and decisions regarding their stakes in the organization.*

Auditing *is an independent review and verification of accounting records.*

Balance sheet *is a financial report that shows the net worth of an organization in the form of assets, liabilities, and owners' equity at a specific point in time.*

Budgeting *is the process of planning and preparing a budget to influence profit in relation to revenue and expenses.*

Budgets *are plans for operating an organization stated in financial terminologies.*

Capital budgets *are the projected amounts planned to be used for capital items in a given period.*

Cash budget *forecasts the cash inflow and outflow expectations for a specific accounting period.*

Cash flow *is a term describing cash receipts (inflows) and cash payments or disbursements (outflows).*

Cash flow statement *is a financial report that shows how much cash is generated, used, and retained by an organization in a specific period.*

Cash inflow *is the cash received by a business entity for products or services sold (e.g., the cash received for food and beverage sales).*

Cash outflow *is the cash paid by a business entity to suppliers for inventories and operating expenses (e.g., the cash paid for food and beverage cost).*

Ceteris paribus *is a term used to refer to "other things equal," basically used to describe a relationship when other conditions of that relationship remain the same.*

Check around competitive pricing *is a pricing strategy in which a hotel can use websites to select a competitive set of hotel rates to be monitored, check out the real-time room rates offered by these hotels, and determine a competitive rate to charge in relation to the hotel's competitive set.*

Consolidated budget *summarizes all the projected revenues, expenses, and net income of the organization for the specified fiscal year.*

Control *can be described as the ability to exercise authority over something, somebody, or a situation in order to attain the anticipated goals.*

Controllable costs *are cost that can be changed in the short term.*

Cost accounting *is a subdivision of managerial accounting that focuses on cost control.*

Cost *is an expense incurred by an organization for the production of goods or for services rendered.*

Cost control *is the process of monitoring costs in order to attain the anticipated financial goal of the organization.*

Cost of sales *is the cost the hospitality establishment paid for the products or the raw materials used to make the products (e.g., food and beverage) that are sold to its customers.*

Cost or expense centers *in the hospitality industry are the staff departments that support the operating departments that generate sales.*

Current assets *are cash and other assets that can be converted into cash within one year (e.g., cash, accounts receivable, inventories, etc.).*

Current liabilities *are debts and other obligations that are less than one year (e.g., accounts payable, tax payable, accrued expenses, etc.).*

Demand (occupancy) *refers to the number of rooms sold.*

Depreciation *is an accounting principle of allocating the cost associated with the purchase of a tangible asset over its estimated useful life.*

External reports *are external performance data on thousands of hotels that could be used to make rate or pricing-related decisions.*

Financial accounting *focuses on reporting an organization's transaction, performance, and financial position to parties outside the organization.*

Financial analysis *is the assessment of a business's monetary affairs, financial statements, budgets, and other finance-related reports for decision-making purposes.*

Financial reporting *is the process of providing financial information to stakeholders outside of the organization.*

Fiscal year *is the twelve-month accounting period used by business organizations. The fiscal year used by most business organizations concurs with the calendar year and ends on December 31.*

Fixed costs *are expenses that remain the same regardless of the sales volume. In other words, fixed costs are unaffected by changes in sales volume.*

Follow the leader pricing *is a pricing strategy in which a hotel sets the rate of its rooms to be the same as its competitive set leader in the area.*

Food and beverage (F&B) cost control *is the process of monitoring F&B costs in order to attain the anticipated financial performance from F&B sales.*

Food and beverage costs *are the expenses incurred by an organization for the purchase of the food and beverage needed for that business.*

Generally accepted accounting principles *are accounting concepts, standard of measurements, and standard of presentation mandated to be used in a financial statement.*

Gross profit *is the difference between revenue and the cost of goods sold.*

Income statement *is a financial report that shows the revenue, expenses, and profit or loss of an organization for a specified time period (e.g., a month, quarter, or year). The income statement is also known as a profit and loss (P&L) statement, earnings statement, or operating statement.*

Internal control *is a way to assure management that the accounting information that is reported via the accounting system is correct and reliable.*

Internal rate of return (IRR) *is an assessment technique used in capital budgeting to analyze the discount rate that makes the net present value of all cash flows from a particular investment or project equal to zero.*

Internal reports *are reports that are generated in a hotel or lodging establishment with the help of PMS or other systems to show the performance of the establishment in regard to the occupancy rate, ADR, RevPAR, etc.*

Labor cost *is the sum of salaries and wages paid to employees including employee benefits and payroll taxes.*

Liquidity *is the amount of available cash or cash equivalents that a business entity has to cover its operating expenses.*

Long-term assets *are an organization's properties and equipment with a period of more than one year useful life remaining (e.g., land, building, etc.).*

Long-term debts *are liabilities and other obligations of a business entity that are longer than a one-year obligation (e.g., mortgage loans, lease obligations, etc.).*

Long-term liabilities *are debts and other obligations of a business entity that are longer than a one-year obligation (e.g., mortgage loans, lease obligations, etc.).*

Managerial accounting *is the identification, analysis, and interpretation of historical and/or projected financial data used to assist management in making daily and future operational plans.*

Net cash flow (closing bank balance) *is the amount left in the bank account of the business entity after balancing the cash flow statement.*

Net present value (NPV) *is an assessment technique used in capital budgeting to analyze the difference between the present value of cash inflows and the present value of cash outflows.*

Net profit after tax *is the total sales (revenue) minus the cost of goods sold (COGS) and all other operating expenses and taxes.*

Non-controllable or **uncontrollable costs** *are costs that cannot be changed in the short term.*

Numbers *are figures used to measure quantities, amounts, or statistical facts. In business, numbers are also used to measure the financial performance of an organization.*

Occupancy forecast *refers to the number of rooms estimated to be sold.*

Occupancy rate *refers to the percentage of rooms sold, which can be computed by dividing the number of rooms sold by the total number of rooms available in the hotel for sale.*

Operating expenses *are the costs of the goods and services utilized to earn revenue (sales).*

Owner's equity *refers to the owner's claim of the resources with economic value, which are expected to provide benefits to future operations.*

Payback period *is the length of time expected to recover the cost of a given investment or project.*

Preparation standard *is the standard procedure for production intended to ensure that each portion of a given product conforms to its standard recipe.*

Prestige pricing *is a pricing strategy in which a hotel sets the rate of its rooms to be the highest rate in a particular area and justifies the rate with a better product and/or services.*

Prime cost *in the hospitality industry refers to the sum of food cost, beverage cost, and payroll and related expenses.*

Pro forma earnings statement *is a projected earnings statement based on rational assumptions, which is usually used in support of a business plan or proposal.*

Rack rate *is the price per room type at which the lodging establishment sells each room when no discounts are offered to any guest.*

Revenue centers *in the hospitality industry are operating departments that produce revenues (sales) by providing products and/or services that generate revenue to clients.*

Revenue *is a term that refers to the total sales.*

Revenue management (RM) *is a tactical approach used to maximize revenues while supplying the same quantity of product.*

Revenue management meeting *can be described as a meeting of an organization's department heads with the purpose of enhancing the organization's revenue management philosophy and garnering the support of the concerned departments and employees.*

Revenue management team refers to individuals who manage the tactics used to maximize revenues.

Revenue manager *is the* individual who manages the tactics used to maximize revenues.

RevPAR *stands for revenue per available room, which can be computed by dividing rooms' revenue by the total number of rooms available in the hotel for sale.*

Solvency *is the ability of a business entity to meet its long-term liabilities and to accomplish long-term expansion.*

Spreadsheet modeling *of financial statements provides a simplified way to use Microsoft Excel or another spreadsheet to design and analyze financial statements.*

Stakeholders *are groups or individuals who have a stake in the form of financial resources, human resources, or another form of assets in an organization or the community where the organization is located.*

Standard portion size can be described as the quantity of a product to be served each time the product is ordered.

Straight-line depreciation *is a depreciating method that recognizes an equal portion of the asset's cost as depreciation expense over the estimated useful life of the asset.*

Supply *refers to the number of rooms available for sale.*

Total cost *is the combination of all unit costs in a given period (i.e., week, month, or year). Total cost can also be described as the sum of variable and fixed costs.*

Unit cost *refers to the expenses associated with a portion of food, beverage, or labor.*

Variable costs *are expenses that vary with changes in output. In other words, variable costs are affected by changes in sales volume.*

Answers to Chapter Review Problems

Chapter 1
1. 75.00%
2. $32,000.00
3. $80.00
4. a = Revenue = $1,916,250.00
   b = Gross Profit = $1,316,250.00
   c = NPBT = $416,250.00
   d = NPAT = $270,562.50
5. $416,250.00
6. 26.00%
7. 4.00%
8. a = Bad because the restaurant sales did not increase as planned in the budget
   b = 15.79%
   c = 5.26%
   d = 9.09%
   e = 1,250 rooms per month
   f = Percentage
   g = 27 cents out of every food revenue dollar is used to pay for the food items/produce

Chapter 3
8. $699,500.00

Chapter 4
1. I. 100.00%
   II. 29.81%
   III. 70.19%
   IV. 49.66%

V. 20.53%

2. I. $110,600.00
II. $35,750.00
III. $74,850.00
IV. $52,293.00
V. $22,557.00

Chapter 5
1. a. $113,237.26
b. $77,107.60
c. $102,107.60
d. $11,129.66
e. $113,237.26

2. II. Total receipt = 102,832.50, total disbursement = $71,338.39, and Net cash flow = $50,996.11

Chapter 6
1. Keys to answer this question: Total sales = $1,420,770.00, total cost of sales = $389,154.00, total gross profit = $1,031,616.00, total operating expenses = $674,930.50
2. $203,619.93
3. a $787,500.00
b. $86,616.00
4. a. $73,500.00
b. $18,405.90

Chapter 7
1. 135,940
2. $31,482,875.00
3. 135,940
4. $34,631,162.50
5. $3,148,287.50
6. 74.49%
7. $231.59
8. $172.51
9. 74.49%
10. $254.75
11. $189.76

Chapter 8

1. a. 6.00%
   b. 8.00%
   c. 10.00%
   d. 12.00%
   e. 20.00%
   f. 24.00%

2. a. $1,750.00
   b. $1,500.00
   c. $1,250.00
   d. $1,000.00
   e. $750.00
   f. $500.00

3. a. $2,000.00
   b. $3,000.00
   c. $5,000.00
   d. $10,000.00
   e. $20,000.00
   f. $50,000.00

4. a. $0.50
   b. $30.00
   c.   I. 10 bottles
        II. $100.00
        III. $0.63

5. a. $1,100,000.00
   b. $238,000.00
   c. $60,000.00
   d. $220,00.00
   e. $55,000.00
   f. $275,000.00

Index

CPSIA information can be obtained
at www.ICGtesting.com
Printed in the USA
LVHW061008050622
720541LV00011B/349